CHRISTMAS

First published in the UK and North America in 2019 by
Ivy Press
An imprint of The Quarto Group
The Old Brewery, 6 Blundell Street
London N7 9BH, United Kingdom
T (0)20 7700 6700 **F** (0)20 7700 8066
www.QuartoKnows.com

British Library Cataloguing-in-Publication Data
A catalogue record for this book is available from
the British Library

ISBN: 978-1-78240-780-5

This book was conceived, designed and produced by
Ivy Press
58 West Street, Brighton BN1 2RA, United Kingdom

Publisher Susan Kelly
Editorial Director Tom Kitch
Art Director James Lawrence
Project Editor Elizabeth Clinton
Design Manager Anna Stevens
Designer Clare Barber
Editorial Assistant Niamh Jones

Printed in China

10 9 8 7 6 5 4 3 2 1

CHRISTMAS

A SHORT HISTORY
FROM SOLSTICE TO SANTA

ANDY THOMAS

IVY PRESS

Contents

Preface

I grew up in a household that very much celebrated Christmas. My parents would send me and my sisters to bed one December night, and the next morning the living room would be mysteriously and magically transformed. I would stare in awe at the wonderfully peculiar fir tree now standing by the window, glowing and scented. This transformation, repeated in countless other homes, announced that, for the next week or two, the world had changed, and life would be different.

In the run-up to each Christmas, my father had a custom of reading Charles Dickens's *A Christmas Carol* to himself as a way of welcoming in the seasonal atmosphere. As we grew old enough to absorb the tale's subtleties, he began to read excerpts to us until eventually I adopted the habit of annually reading it myself for a number of years. Dickens's atmospheric vision of foggy shadows and bright joy left its mark on me.

Decades went by, and my life embraced authoring and lecturing on unexplained phenomena and hidden histories. I never lost my love for Christmas and, as I became drawn to investigate folklore traditions, I wanted to know more about the festive season. I discovered in its past a rich seam of overlapping cultures, a complex history of intrigue, and a whole cauldron of different meanings. Yet all were essentially celebrations of light over darkness. In a sometimes difficult and unpredictable world, this has always been important.

As I began to find myself spending each November and December giving live presentations that attempted to express all of this, I was increasingly asked if I had written a book that took the same approach. Here, then, is the answer to those requests.

While deliberately concise in its format, I have tried to be inclusive and respectful to the different beliefs and numerous global traditions, and I hope this will encourage readers to reassess a celebration that, in these days of overt commercialization, sometimes gets a bad press. Christmas is far more than plastic Santas and shopping sprees, and it can still have great meaning for us today if approached in the right spirit.

Christmas and its ancient alternatives have seen many modes of expression around the world, although certain countries have taken the lead in setting and resetting the form over the centuries. There is, then, an inevitable emphasis on

Great Britain, Scandinavia, Germany, and North America, but ancient Egyptians and Romans also feature, and I have tried to cast my net wide. Some material will be familiar, but I have highlighted some unsung areas of the season that may surprise some readers, and I devote a few extra pages to the Puritan ban on the festivities in the mid-1600s, because it emphasizes, for the Scrooge-sympathizers in our society, what happens when Christmas *is* taken away, and why we should value such important celebrations.

Bring on the seasonal cheer, then, as we journey through the multiple guises and the many wonders of Christmas.

Andy Thomas

Introduction

As mid-December approaches in Western countries, a special atmosphere sets in. The weather and light have a feeling all of their own, and by way of acknowledgment, people start mounting a festival that has been with us, in some form or another, since ancient times. They put up colorful lights and sparkling objects to illuminate the gloom, hunt for gifts that might please loved ones, encourage good cheer, extend a spirit of goodwill beyond the usual boundaries, and plan meals on a scale rarely attempted in any other season, as if in willful defiance of winter's steely austerity. Soon everything orbits around this outlandish and yet compellingly magnificent celebration.

So where did all this glorious madness come from? Why do we do what we do at Christmas?

When we alter the environment around us, we are, of course, making a powerful statement; that we want to behave differently and feel different during this period. We are drawing a line in the sand from the rest of the year and declaring our intention to enter a state of mind where celebration takes the place of anxiety, and being nice to ourselves and to others is allowed just a little more than usual. We have entered the Christmas zone, where normal rules no longer apply.

So many decorations light up, or hold echoes of nature: radiant stars, reflective orbs, snowflakes, and strips of tinsel on a richly adorned tree recalling frost-covered branches. Christmas celebrations evolved in the Northern Hemisphere, where December is a cold, dark time of year with nature at its most dormant—and so people remind themselves of its beauty even in the harshest times and cherish every little glow they can find. It is a festival of light in the darkness.

To celebrate is to be human and, whether we consciously know it or not, each of us is deeply rooted in the old ceremonies, beliefs, and rituals of earlier cultures. By looking back at the legends and at how this winter feast day has grown and evolved over the years, we can better understand ourselves and know just why so many are raising a glass and wishing everyone a "Merry Christmas" in rooms full of strange but beautiful paraphernalia. One way or another, people have been doing this for a long time.

CHAPTER ONE
ANCIENT CHRISTMAS

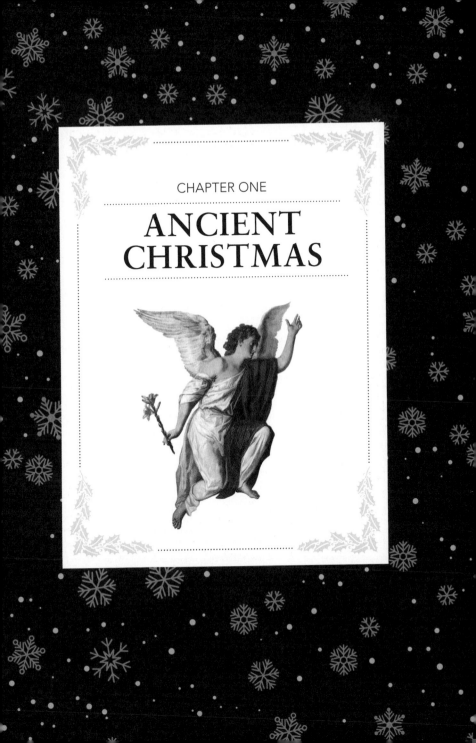

Ancient Celebrations

It is a simple truth that long before Christmas became Christmas, there were midwinter festivals across the Northern Hemisphere around what modern calendars now call December 25. The very word "seasonal," which can often refer to Christmas, draws our minds to a stark awareness that we live on a tilted, spinning globe that revolves around the sun, exposing the north to more sunlight in summer and less in winter and leaving its inhabitants with harsh, icy beauty or depressing, misty dullness in the dark days of December.

To the ancients, whose existence hung on the moods of the weather, recording the movements of what they saw in the heavens was crucial. It was their only guide to understanding and predicting the seasonal cycles. So they built temples that, as far as we can see, served both ceremonial and practical purposes. Whatever else some of the bigger stone circles and complexes of Europe might have been, they also appear to have served as seasonal clocks,

recording, in particular, the solstices (see page 15), marking the extreme ends of the earth's elliptical procession around the sun, from summer to winter and back.

Until recently, it was assumed that England's famous Stonehenge monument in Wiltshire was orientated around midsummer. Recent discoveries, however, suggest its original users visited it primarily at the winter solstice. The huge stones have alignments to both seasons' skies, but midwinter appears to have mattered more; some say the tallest stone is placed to point directly to the midwinter sunrise. It seems that knowing when the sun would begin its first small steps back toward full strength mattered more to them than celebrating its summer glory.

BELOW: England's famous Stonehenge monument was a major gathering place for ancient peoples at both solstices—but the midwinter sunrise was the key event.

The Winter Solstice

Even today, people gather at England's Stonehenge and other Neolithic complexes around the world to mark the solstices—and the importance to the ancients of the winter turning point is becoming clearer. Newgrange in Ireland, for instance, was built to let beams from the midwinter sunrise strike the back of the burial chamber. But understanding what "solstice" actually means gives a stronger clue to why we celebrate Christmas when we do.

"Solstice" is derived from the Latin words *sol* (sun) and *sistere* (to stand still), and so literally translates as "the sun stands still." This describes perfectly what happens to the sun as we see it in the sky, usually on December 21 or 22. (The drift of date is due to small orbital variations; occasionally it can go forward to December 23 or fall back to December 20.) At this point in the earth's orbit, the heavens appear to pause. Thus, what the naked eye sees for three days or so from the winter solstice is the sun rising and setting in effectively identical places. But then, around December 25, positions begin to change and the sun starts its new cycle toward lighter days.

For the ancients, this was a momentous time, because it meant they could now definitively look forward to life becoming just that little bit more survivable again. Somewhere in our bones, we still feel that joy.

A celebration of light in the darkness at this time of year raises its head in many cultures. A few examples of near equivalents to Christmas include Dongzhi (Chinese), Hanukkah (Judaic), Korochun (Slavic), Makar Sankranti (Hindu), Yalda (Iranian), Yule (Germanic/Norse—see page 43), and Ziemassvētki (Latvian). They all revolve around the same jubilant fact: the sun has begun its slow curve back, so summer and warmth will return, crops will grow, and nature will be abundant once again.

Sol Invictus & Saturnalia

Before Germanic Yule festivities entered the picture, Christmas was greatly influenced by Roman beliefs. Much of Europe and North Africa were once part of that empire, and its pagan traditions had a surprising influence on the Christian holiday. In fact, in addition to Jesus, a number of significant deities from antiquity are said to share December 25 as their ceremonial birthday.

OTHER DEITIES

Some say that the Roman sun god, Sol Invictus (the "unconquered sun"), or Helios to the Greeks, was a deity who celebrated his birthday on or around December 25, and that the early Christians simply adopted the same *Dies Natalis Solis Invicti* festival for Jesus. Depictions of Christ from earlier times do often carry overt sun god symbolism, with the halo believed by some researchers to be a derivation of sun rays. However, a number of scholars believe that the adoption of the date was coincidental, used for its evident positive connotations but no more; it has even been argued that the use of December 25 for Jesus might predate the Sol Invictus festival, which is not clearly recorded before 274 CE.

Mithras, originally a Persian god, was another popular Roman deity in the first centuries, especially among soldiers, because it was believed that following the rites of Mithras made for a smoother passage to the afterlife. Mithras is also sometimes associated with December 25, although this might be a historical blending with Sol Invictus, who plays a role in the Mithras story. The Egyptian god Horus may also have a connection with the winter solstice (see page 18).

RIGHT: The mythology of the Roman god Mithras, often depicted sacrificing a bull, features the sun god Sol Invictus, whose birthday was on or around December 25.

ABOVE: *Saturnalia* by Antoine Callet. This prominent Roman festival, though rather more risqué than later celebrations, would heavily influence Christmas traditions.

Some claim that almost every ancient god had a December 25 birthday, but academic study suggests this is too sweeping a statement. What is for certain, though, is that the visual depiction of Sol Invictus, complete with halo, was picked up and transferred seamlessly to the early Roman depictions of Jesus, and that Roman festivals, especially Saturnalia and the New Year Kalendae, helped form many Christmas traditions.

CELEBRATING SATURNALIA & KALENDAE

Saturnalia, held December 17–23, was a joyous and sometimes debauched remembrance of the "golden age" of the god Saturn (Kronos in Greece), when people enjoyed the earth's bounty in a state of prehistoric innocence. Saturnalia involved much drinking, partying, and even role reversal, where the normal order was subverted; householders might serve their slaves meals on this day instead of the other way around. Masters of ceremonies, or *Saturnalicius princeps*, would be appointed to direct the unbounded festivities, ensuring guaranteed merriment. Remnants of all this mischief would resurface in the later medieval Christmas "misrule" events (see page 60).

Saturnalia, albeit in a toned-down form, would leave an enduring legacy, but it was not the only precursor from Rome. The solar New Year Kalendae (or Kalends, the opening of a Roman month) followed Saturnalia on January 1–3. The giving of gifts, usually delicacies, such as pastries, figs, and honey, was one such custom, beginning a seasonal tradition of reaching out to others that remains today. Revealingly, the fourth–century chronicler Libanius recorded some of the customs of the January Kalendae:

> *The feast of the Kalendae is honored as far as the Roman Empire stretches . . . Everywhere is singing and feasting; the rich enjoy luxury but the poor also set better food than usual upon their tables. The desire to spend money grips everybody . . . People are not merely bountiful to themselves but to their fellow humans. A stream of presents pours itself out on all sides . . . The Kalendae bring all work to a halt, and allow humans to surrender themselves to pure pleasure.*

This quote could easily describe modern Christmas! Although the context may have evolved, it is clear that not much has really changed.

Mother & Child

Although an increasingly secular and multicultural approach has gradually reworked the meaning of what we celebrate at this time of year, Christmas in the West is still primarily associated with the birth of Jesus. Yet the traditional biblical tale of humble beginnings and the vengeance of King Herod has some fascinating earlier precedents in ancient Egyptian mythology.

In these myths, the great goddess Isis and her god-man son Horus are forced to flee the tyrant Set, who is intent on killing him. Horus spends his early life hiding in Egypt, as does Jesus, hiding from Herod. The fourth-century Cypriot bishop Epiphanius of Salamis noted in his work *Panarion* (in the context of listing various pagan heresies) that the life of Horus was celebrated by ancient Egyptians at the winter solstice.

Statuettes of Isis, Horus, and his father Osiris suggest a compelling prototype of the "Holy Family" of Mary, Joseph, and Jesus, while many scholars see a direct lineage from the depictions of Isis and the suckling Horus to the iconography of the sacred mother and child seen so often in the Nativity's Madonna and Child imagery. Occasional statues and paintings of Madonnas with black skin may just represent regional interpretations, but they are considered by some to be echoes of black Isis statues, or even pagan goddesses such as Demeter and Ceres.

As a side note, it has been pointed out that a number of Egyptian deities had the name

"Meri" (as translated phonetically) attached to their names. Meri meant "beloved," so Isis is sometimes referred to as Isis-Meri, leading some observers to wonder if there might be a connection here to the name Mary. This has been dismissed as probable coincidence in academic circles, but the debate keeps internet forums busy.

Such tales may feel a long way from a modern Christmas, but they show the universality of sacred images of a mother and baby. These ancient stories do not weaken, but strengthen, the impact of the later Nativity story as a restatement of sacred truths.

LEFT: An ancient Egyptian statuette of the goddess Isis and her son Horus. Sacred mother and baby symbolism recurs throughout history. Isis's crown comprises a sun-disk and cow horns.

RIGHT: A nineteenth-century Russian icon of the Virgin Mary and Jesus. Such depictions have very likely evolved from their ancient predecessors.

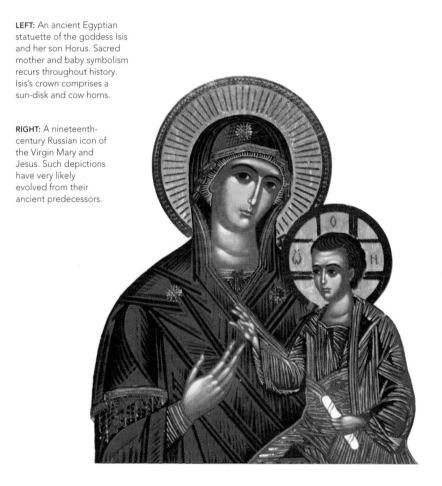

The Nativity Story

For centuries, in Christian countries, children were brought up with the tale of the Nativity at the heart of Christmas. The details are recorded in the Bible gospels of Luke and Matthew (which give slightly different accounts), and a version also appears in the Quran. Whether taken literally or symbolically, the story retains its power.

Most people are aware of the fundamental elements, usually compressed together from the two gospels, mainly from Matthew's longer account. A woman named Mary from Nazareth (now in modern Israel), is visited by an angel named Gabriel, who tells her she is to bear the new Son of God. She subsequently conceives a child through the intercession of the Holy Spirit. With her betrothed husband-to-be Joseph, now more understanding of her surprise pregnancy after receiving his own message from an angel in a dream, they marry as planned, and the expectant Mary travels to Bethlehem to be part of a Roman census, because it is the city of the House of David from which Joseph is descended. Her child is born in Bethlehem, but finding nowhere to stay, the

baby Jesus has to be laid in a manger. Nearby shepherds receive the news of the momentous birth from a host of angels and arrive to worship the child.

Later, wise men from the east come to visit, having followed a star that has alerted them to seek the new "King of the Jews." Consulting the tyrannical King Herod about the whereabouts of the child on the way, they inadvertently alert him to what he sees as a potential threat, and he takes the extreme precautionary measure of ordering the massacre of all the male children of Bethlehem under two years old. Alerted by another angel after visiting Jesus, the wise men secretly return home without giving Herod any further information, and Mary and Joseph flee with the newborn Jesus to Egypt, where he spends his early life.

Given some of the adult themes of the Nativity narrative, it is perhaps surprising that children have been reenacting it in churches or school plays for many years. Tears and laughter over who gets to be a shepherd and who gets to be a king can distract from the story's dark side. Yet its symbolism retains a fascination that keeps people coming back to it.

It is not known whether the events recorded in the gospels really occurred as described (for when it might have occurred, see page 30), or whether they were deliberate reassertions of earlier sacred symbolism that would have been meaningful to the people of the early centuries, giving credence to the new Christian religion. As written, the account picks up on a number of Old Testament prophecies and revives themes from the story of Moses in particular (for example, the mass killing of children), but elements of the birth of Horus may also be present.

Historical corroboration is light. Luke tells us that the events took place in Judea in the reign of Caesar Augustus (27 BCE to 14 CE), which gives some orientation, but there are no clear records of a Roman census in Judea around this time. This seems unusual for an occupying force strict on recording administrative detail. The only reference is a much later mention by the Jewish historian Josephus. Nor is there any contemporary note of Herod's massacre of the innocents (told only by Matthew), not even from sources that held him in low regard. Yet Herod is a known historical figure, and it is hard to prove that it *didn't* happen.

LEFT: Mary, Joseph, and the infant Jesus make the "flight to Egypt," where Jesus would be brought up, to escape the murderous intentions of King Herod.

Mangers & Stables

A carol often sung by children, suited as it is with its friendly tones and sweet sentiments, is "Away in a Manger," which acknowledges something central to the story of Jesus's birth. The song evokes a baby born in a stable, with lowing cattle and other animals around him, from donkeys to lambs. Interestingly, however, and to the surprise of some, a stable is never directly referred to in the Bible.

Some gnostic sources give the birthplace as a cave (which has echoes of the Mithras story, because he was said to have been born directly from the rock of a cave, in another unconventional conception and birth). The Bible reports that there was "no room at the inn" for the Holy Family and that the baby was laid in a manger, but where the manger was and what kind it might have been is unspecified. Farmyard animals are not mentioned at all.

The customary symbolism makes a powerful statement, however, regardless of one's religious beliefs. This important figure, born in the humblest of surroundings, is one of us. His wisdom will not be unreachable, understandable to only the chosen few, but available to all. This is reinforced by the notable detail that the first people to be told of the birth of the Son of God are a group of everyday shepherds, bringing things usefully down to earth. Overwhelmed by visions of angels and the knowledge that they have been selected before all others to hear the good news, they become the first visitors to the holy child, thus immortalizing their profession forever in endless artworks and dramatizations.

What, however, of the wise men from the east, so often shown (probably erroneously) rubbing shoulders with the shepherds in the stable? Who were they, and where did they come from?

Nativity cribs

Decorative cribs for the home seem to have evolved from the popular staging of live Nativity tableaus using actors and animals, first recorded when Saint Francis of Assisi arranged one in Italy in 1223. Francis was deeply moved by the humility of the child in the manger. Setting such an image before the "bodily eyes" of his fellow Christians, he reasoned, would call to mind the hardships Christ had willingly suffered for their sakes, and thus deepen their love for "the Babe of Bethelehem."

The Magi

The wise men, or "three kings," of the Nativity only appear in Matthew's gospel and are often referred to as "the Magi" (from where we get the word "magic"), which derives from the name of a priestly caste of the Persian Zoroastrian religion. This tells us something of their probable origin. Along with the startling fact that the Bible doesn't mention a stable, another amazement to many people is that Matthew never specifies how many wise men

there were and doesn't at any point describe them as kings. These descriptions are later traditions that gradually seeped in. How soon it was after Jesus's birth that the Magi arrived to worship him is also contentious (see page 32).

Some Eastern churches give the number of wise men as twelve, perhaps suggesting an allegorical connection to the twelve signs of the zodiac. The popular depiction of three appears to be inferred from the description of

BELOW: *Adoration of the Magi*, by Petr Maixner (1872). This is a classic depiction of the "three wise men," yet the Bible never numbers or names them. These details are later additions.

the Magi's three gifts, suggesting the same number of givers, and trinities are repeating themes in Christianity and other mystic traditions. The exact same gifts of gold, frankincense (incense), and myrrh (an embalming oil) given to Jesus were said to have been also presented by the Syrian king Seleucus II Callinicus at the Temple of Apollo at Miletus in 243 BCE, suggesting an earlier precedent. The perceived symbolism of the gifts to the future life of Jesus is embodied in the carol "We Three Kings."

The elevation of the wise men to kings, traditionally named Balthazar, Caspar, and Melchior (with several other variations; they are never named in the Bible), seems to have been the creation of later thinkers seeking to link to prophecies in the Old Testament. Notable among them is Psalm 72:10, which states, "Yea, all kings shall fall down before him: all nations serve him." Old depictions of Saint Nicholas (whom we will meet later) baptizing three pagan kings may also have influenced the legends.

There may be yet another Egyptian Nativity connection to consider, which might tell us more about the "three kings" terminology. It has been suggested that some of the gospel stories may embody astronomical or astrological allegory. The Magi are clearly described as astrologers, following a star that leads them to find the King of the Jews. Could it be, though, aside from other possible zodiac links, that the three kings may be stars themselves?

In recent decades, a view has grown among some archeologists that the three main pyramids placed in a line on the famous Giza Plateau near Cairo in Egypt, ordered to be built one by one by the three kings of Khufu, Khafre, and Menkaure, may have been aligned to directly mirror the three stars in the belt at the center of the distinctive constellation Orion—which are also named the "three kings" in some mythologies and star charts (for example, by the Dutch and Afrikaners). The smallest star in Orion's belt is slightly out of line with the others, and the smallest pyramid is, too; this leads some observers to believe that the ancients were trying, literally, to recreate heaven on earth.

To the Egyptians, Orion was Osiris, father of Horus, and the bright star of nearby Sirius represented Isis. In some Christian traditions, however, Orion has become associated with John the Baptist, herald of Jesus. To this day, scholars and mystics find great satisfaction in tracing overlaps and echoes of Egyptian symbolism in the Nativity story.

RIGHT: The constellation Orion, associated with John the Baptist in some traditions, has three distinctive stars in its "belt," sometimes called the "three kings."

BELOW: The main Egyptian pyramids at Giza, Cairo, ordered to be built by three kings. Some archeologists believe they were arranged to mirror the stars in Orion's belt.

ORION'S BELT

The Star of Bethlehem

The most obvious astronomical feature of the Nativity is the Star of Bethlehem, or "Christmas star," the symbol of which adorns the tops of festive trees to this day. What was the actual "star of wonder" that the wise men were said to be following? There has been much speculation in all kinds of academic circles.

Like the Magi themselves, the Star of Bethlehem, as it is often referred to, appears in only the Bible's Gospel of Matthew. If it wasn't literally a miraculous phenomenon, as some Christians still believe, what else could explain this aerial sign? While "ancient aliens" aficionados have suggested the likes of spaceships, some astronomers have considered it a straightforward reference to the bright star of Sirius (Isis to the Egyptians, remember) that travelers would sometimes use to guide them across plains and deserts, rising as it does in the east and then moving west relatively low in the sky within the course of a single night.

Some historians dismiss the star completely as a narrative fiction designed to create significance around the birth of Jesus at a time when astrological signs would have been seen as highly meaningful. For a religion that would later shun astrology, Christianity began by apparently embracing it. But many researchers have looked for a more tangible candidate for the Christmas star. If we take as probable poetic license the description of it moving but then coming to a halt over the exact birthplace of Jesus, there are a number of interesting possibilities to consider. If we accept that Matthew was referring to *something* visible in the sky, then what else might the Star of Bethlehem have been?

Signs in the Sky

There are many phenomena that have been interpreted as signs in the sky. It is notable that in 66 CE, around the time Matthew's gospel was being written, the regular visitor Halley's Comet (which arrives in our celestial neighborhood every seventy-five years or so) was bright in the sky, coinciding with the arrival of a delegation of magi in Rome. Did this give Matthew an inspiration?

Other comets, or even supernovae (impressively bright exploding stars, one of which may have been recorded in 5 BCE), have been suggested as further potential stars, although there is nothing particularly overt recorded by astronomers around that time. Halley's Comet had also been spectacular in 12 BCE, but this seems too early a date for the Nativity.

It is generally agreed by scholars that Jesus was born slightly earlier than when 1 BC became 1 AD. This is a little counterintuitive, because BC stands for "before Christ" and AD for *anno Domini* (medieval Latin for "in the year of the Lord")—although in the modern era, the more secular terms BCE (before common era) and CE (common era) are increasingly preferred. However, King

Herod is generally believed to have died in 4 BCE. An alternative date for his death is 1 BCE, but even so, Matthew mentions him as an active participant in the story, so, Jesus can't have been born as late as the year 1 CE.

There is a tantalizing possibility that the description of a star may actually refer to a coming together (conjunction) of planets instead, which can be spectacular. If later dates for Herod's death are considered, the conjunction of Jupiter and Venus in 3 BCE or the three conjunctions of Jupiter and the star Regulus in 2 BCE, might be contenders for the Star of Bethlehem. However, there has been much speculation that three conjunctions of Saturn and Jupiter in Pisces in 7 BCE—a date which some researchers believe is nearer to the real birth of Jesus—might have been seen as especially portentous. With many modern astrologers seeing the era of Jesus as being the beginning of the Age of Pisces, and given that this zodiac sign is represented by two fish—fish symbolism eventually coming to represent Christianity—it may be that these conjunctions in Pisces became misremembered as a star. It has even been suggested that the common placements of the characters in Nativity scenes may be deliberately encoded depictions of the sky in 7 BCE. There may certainly be more astronomical meaning embedded into the Biblical story than is at first apparent.

LEFT: Halley's Comet, photographed by W. Liller in 1986. It is one candidate of inspiration for the inclusion of a Christmas "star" in the Nativity story.

Epiphany

The Epiphany (Greek for "manifestation" or "appearance") is the day that now generally commemorates the arrival of the wise men. When they might have turned up, however, has been much debated. If the signs that alerted them were the conjunctions of 7 BCE (see page 31) or other alignments in this period, no one knows how long they spent in preparation before journeying to Bethlehem. For convenient shorthand, they are often shown arriving shortly after the birth in the stable with the shepherds, but Matthew simply says they came "after Jesus had been born"; some traditions suggest as much as two or more years after.

Most Western Christianity uses January 6 to celebrate Epiphany, marking the first liturgical period after the Twelve Days of Christmas (see page 40). However, confusion can arise depending on where one lives. Due to their continued adherence to the old Julian (Roman) calendar, instead of the modern Gregorian system introduced by Pope Gregory XIII in 1582, some Eastern

ABOVE: Befana, a crotchety old woman celebrated in Italian folklore at the Epiphany, seen here in an 1840 image from the Parisian journal *Magasin Pittoresque*.

Orthodox churches have January 6–7 as Christmas itself, with Epiphany on January 19. Different dates altogether are used in some regions, adding further complexity.

Epiphany is a big event in several countries. In many Spanish-speaking nations, this day or its eve sees the three kings (costumed men) arriving with much jollity, throwing candies to children and dispensing gifts, not unlike Santa Claus. In Italy, La Befana, a witchlike old woman (who failed to help the wise men because she was too busy cleaning) is celebrated. Befana is also said to deliver presents (by way of penance) and enters houses through chimneys, thumping with her broomstick anyone who dares to observe her. Russia has the similar figure of Babouschka. Befana is seemingly derived from the Greek word for Epiphany, *epifania*, but she also possibly originates from the old Roman deity Strenia (or Strenua), a goddess of the New Year.

WHAT DOES EPIPHANY CELEBRATE?

Confusing Christmastide calendars even further, the arrival of the Magi was not what the Epiphany always represented. To many early Christians, January 6 was as much seen as commemorating the baptism of Jesus by John in the Jordan River (an important moment, because it was Jesus's first public appearance). Others even saw it as marking Jesus's first reported miracle, when he turned water into wine at the wedding at Cana.

For a while, Epiphany was frequently held as being more important than Jesus's ceremonial birthday of December 25. What unites the varying themes of Epiphany, whether seen as his baptism, first miracle, or acknowledgment by the Magi, is that they all demonstrate his first official presentation to the world.

If the celebration of the baptism of Jesus was threatening to eclipse his birthday in some regions, it is perhaps of note that the birthday of John was subsequently superimposed onto the pagan midsummer festivities. Because these were big in northern Europe and Scandinavia, the change gave John his own separate feast day and allowed for Jesus's birthday to shine a little more. Thus was created a neat cyclical Christian journey, celebrating John's heralding of Jesus at midsummer and culminating in the messiah's actual manifestation at midwinter as "the light of the world" finally piercing into the darkness through the metaphor of the sun beginning its journey back to midsummer, and so on ad infinitum.

CHAPTER TWO

THE BEGINNINGS OF CHRISTMAS

The Beginnings of Christmas

By the time the Roman emperor Constantine unexpectedly decided to adopt Christianity as the official state religion in 380 CE—a huge reversal after centuries of persecution—the celebration that would become known as Christmas (from the Old English, literally meaning "Christs's Mass") was already becoming established. Whether Constantine genuinely believed in the burgeoning religion (he was baptized only shortly before his death after years of murder and tyranny) or just used its newness to political advantage is still debated, but the effect was the same. The Roman gods began to recede or were merged with Jesus and the growing pantheon of Christian martyr-saints, and a new era had begun. No one had foreseen such a huge shift.

Although earlier references can be found to December 25 having been adopted as the birthday of Jesus (a celebration in his honor is described as occurring in Rome in 336 CE), the first acknowledgment that it had become a fully fledged feast day can be found in *The Chronography of 354*, produced, as one might imagine, in 354 CE. Also sometimes known as *The Calendar of Philocalus* in it the Roman scribe Furius Dionysius

RIGHT: A Turkish mosaic from 944 CE showing Mary and the Christchild, flanked by Roman Emperor Constantine on the right, and Emperor Justinian on the left.

Filocalus (Philocalus) notes that not only is December 25 the birthday of the unconquered Sol Invictus Sun god (see page 15), but is also the date that "Christ is born in Bethlehem, Judea." A justification for celebrating both could be found in the Biblical book of Malachi 4:2, with Jesus seen as the prophezied "Sun of righteousness" that will "arise with healing in his wings." The seeds of Christmas as we know it had been sown.

The Advent of Advent

The word "Advent" comes from the Latin, meaning "coming," and the celebration dates back to around 480 CE. In fact, it began as a seasonal equivalent to Lent; also known as the Nativity Fast, in its early years it was a cycle of abstinence and penance, building up to the final festive release. Since then, it has changed a great deal, with cultures around the world celebrating it according to their own dates and practices.

In the West, the season is usually marked with special advent calendars. These date back to the nineteenth century; their doors traditionally conceal a tiny picture, but since the middle of the twentieth century, some manufacturers have also offered a daily chocolate. Although enjoyable, eating candy every day is perhaps not in the spirit of the original fast.

Some practices still remain that are closer to the spiritual roots of the holiday. The German tradition of lighting candles in a wreath each Advent Sunday is an example; in Sweden, this custom also embraces the martyr Saint Lucia's Day on December 13. More elaborately presented candles are sometimes mounted in fruit known as Christingles, meaning "Christ lights," which are carried by children. An alternative is to carry a candle while meditatively walking around a spiral made of greenery. These rituals take the soul through a cycle of anticipation toward the eventual manifestation of Jesus on December 24, the official end of Advent (confusing many a child looking for a calendar window on Christmas Day itself, although some manufacturers have craftily, if controversially, started adding one to compensate).

Epiphany at first was widely seen as the more important festival, so Christmas itself would not become the main event for some centuries. Some early Christians were resistant to even acknowledging it until arguments broke out against the Gnostics, who asserted that Jesus never had a physical body but was a more ethereal presence. Emphasizing the Christmas story, with the build up of Advent, reaffirmed the notion that Christ *was* born into our physical everyday world, thus making him a more reachable figure who sacrificed himself to save humankind from sin, now the central belief of Christianity.

A Joyful Yuletide.

The Twelve Days of Christmas

Early Christians had endless debates among themselves, including arguing over which feast days mattered most. Christmas and Easter eventually became the main poles of the year, but there were Epiphany adherents to appease and the Christmas period had become a mish-mash of Christian and pagan traditions. Hence, in 567 CE, a council of what was now known as "Roman Catholic" leaders ("Catholic" derived from the Greek for "universal") came together in Tours. The city was already an established seat of Christianity in central France and would hold a number of councils over the years, but the 567 event is the one that set the template for the festivities that would follow.

THE TWELVE DAYS

Day 1: December 25—The Nativity (***Christmas Day***)

Day 2: December 26—St. Stephen (***Boxing Day***)

Day 3: December 27—St. John the Evangelist

Day 4: December 28—Feast of the Holy Innocents
(Herod's victims)

Day 5: December 29—St. Thomas Becket

Day 6: December 30—St. Egwin of Worcester

Day 7: December 31—Pope St. Sylvester (***New Year's Eve***)

Day 8: January 1—The Solemnity of Mary, Mother of God

Day 9: January 2—St. Basil the Great and
St. Gregory Nazianzen

Day 10: January 3—Feast of the Holy Name of Jesus

Day 11: January 4—St. Elizabeth Ann Seton and
St. Simon Stylites

Day 12: January 5—St. John Neumann; also St. Edward
the Confessor (UK) and St. Julian the Hospitaller
(***Twelfth Night***)

To build a sensible order around Christmas and Epiphany and end the arguments about which event was most important, it was decreed that a twelve-day sequence of Holy Days, commemorating relevant saints and notable events, would begin on December 25 and end on Twelfth Night, the day before Epiphany, in one unified festal cycle. This period would become known as The Twelve Days of Christmas and evolve further over time.

As is always the way, debates began bubbling almost instantly. Should the twelve days commence on December 25 itself (as per the official decree) or the day after? Should the cycle be based on the Eastern Julian or Western Gregorian calendar? The twelve days never commenced on Christmas Eve, however, despite the fact that many countries in Europe have their gift giving and feasting that day, leaving December 25 free for more religious observations.

The Twelve Days of Christmas—or Christmastide—would in time give rise to many kinds of observances across different countries, as saints and feasts found their own regional resonances. On what much of the West now knows as New Year's Eve, for instance, some nations still celebrate Saint Sylvester's Day. Sylvester reigned as Pope from 314 to 355 CE and little else is known of him, but many countries still remember him with ceremonies of light at midnight masses, fireworks, mask wearing, lentil and sausage eating, and, oddly but sweetly, the parading of pigs on leashes (in Germany and Austria) for reasons now obscure. As Christianity spread around the world through European colonial influence, so too did Christmas, adding further local customs to the Twelve Days.

The Evolution of Christmastide

Soon after the central Roman Empire collapsed (around the fifth century), the power of the Roman Catholic Church effectively replaced it, and it is here that the observance of Christmas as we know it really began. Winter celebrations were nothing new under Roman rule, but under the authority of the Church, Christmas, which had begun as one of the more minor festivals of the ecclesiastical calendar, began to take hold as a key event.

By the Early Middle Ages (also called the Dark Ages, spanning the sixth to tenth centuries), the extended Christmastide period was rapidly returning to the season's pre-Christian roots—which meant a fantastic excuse for two weeks of merriment and feasting. Full religious elements were maintained, but bawdy remnants of Saturnalia and other solstice celebrations remained alive and well, and were perhaps even growing, to the disapproval of the devout.

By now, Christmas Day was seen as important enough to be used to make a point. Kings who wanted to establish themselves as true heirs to a grand tradition often picked it for their coronation days. The great Frankish king Charlemagne, for instance, had himself crowned Emperor of the Romans by Pope Leo III in Rome on Christmas Day in 800. England's Edmund the Martyr, meanwhile, was anointed King of East Anglia on December 25, 855, while, more famously, the Norman invader William the Conqueror was crowned King of the whole of England at Westminster Abbey on Christmas Day 1066 (where cheering crowds outside were mistaken for rioters and chaos reigned as soldiers went on a retributional spree, somewhat spoiling the Christmas atmosphere).

Christmas and monarchs were becoming each others' best allies. It became ever more important to record where they were and what they were doing during the festive period—and, indeed, fans of British royalty still inherit this tradition in the form of the monarch speaking to the nation via television at 3 p.m. every Christmas Day. Rulers used Christmas to promote themselves—and in doing so, promoted Christmas. Gradually its prominence increased, finally eclipsing or absorbing Epiphany in many countries.

Yule & the Wild Hunt

With the proliferation of the Germanic peoples (generally seen as encompassing much of northern Europe and Scandinavia) in the twilight of the Roman Empire, the influence of their Norse mythology, with its own pantheon of gods and customs, began to spread, even as Christianity was welling up in competition.

Each winter, it was believed that the great god Odin would lead the Wild Hunt across the sky, a dark and rowdy supernatural chase of otherworldly beings. Belief in this, together with the marking of the solstice, gave rise to a major festive period that took place between mid-November and early January. The hunt might have astronomical or astrological connotations—some even say paranormal—but unfortunately, its origins are lost in the mists of time. The peoples of that era would have known Odin by

Yule goat

The Yule goat, or Joulupukki, is a Scandinavian emblem taking many guises, either representing the god Thor's chariot pullers or an ethereal presence that arrives shortly before Yule to ensure successful celebrations. The goat is also, of course, the symbol for the zodiac sign of Capricorn, in which the winter solstice takes place. The Yule goat fulfilled the Santa role as the gift giver for a while in some countries, such as Finland, although boisterous men would sometimes dress as goats (in an echo of wassailing—see page 52) and actually demand gifts at people's doors. Straw goats of all sizes remain popular Christmas ornaments in Scandinavian regions today.

several names, such as Wŏden or Wŏdan, but also others based around the word *Jól* (from where the word "jolly" is at least partially derived). The celebrations would thus become anglicized as "Yule," a term many people still use to describe the Christmas period. Indeed, Odin's flying across the sky has probably influenced one of our most important Christmas mythologies (see page 109).

Another Norse-related event from these times was Modraniht (Old English for "Night of the Mothers"), a rare celebration of revered female godlike entities, such as the *dísir*. Held on December 24, and with probable fertility implications, it may also have left its mark on Christmas, albeit, as was unfortunately often the case, with some of the feminine aspect removed. However, the figures of the Italian Befana, who we have already discussed, and the Slavic snow maiden Snegurochka (see page 123), are rare female seasonal characters who survive today.

Merged with the Roman and Christian elements, the Yule traditions have permeated much of what we still do around Christmas. We may no longer

sacrifice animals and splash their blood on our faces and walls (depending on how good we are at carving the turkey), but many of us still drink more alcohol than at other times; in the 900s the Norwegian king, Haakon I, even passed a law requiring all people to drink ale at Yuletide or pay a fine. The Yule log, too, remains to this day, even if it has shrunk to a chocolate cake for most.

Original Yule logs, first officially recorded in 1134 but suspected by some observers to have much earlier pagan origins, were huge blocks of wood that would slowly burn for the whole of Yuletide. A remnant would be kept as a good luck charm throughout the year—it could apparently ward off toothache and chilblains—before being used to light the new log the following year. Exactly what kind of wood made up this log varied from nation to nation. English celebrants favored oak, ash, or pine; French people tended to go for fruit trees; while in Florence, it was olive wood. Sparks arising from the log were generally seen as a good omen for the coming year.

The aforementioned King Haakon was one of the first Norse kings to become Christian, as the growing religion's traveling evangelists had ever-more success, and he made a conscious effort to seamlessly unite Yule and Christmas. It would appear he succeeded, and the Normans—descended directly from Vikings—further reinforced the merging in Great Britain when they swept across it from 1066.

Medieval Christmas

The term "medieval" technically describes the thousand years between the fifth and fifteenth centuries (the Middle Ages) and is thus nebulous in its sweep. To most people, the nostalgic collective image of medieval Christmas usually means allegedly chivalric knights, finely dressed ladies, tapestries, and castles, with kings throwing poultry bones over their shoulders during the seasonal feast. Insofar as such a time ever really existed, we are probably thinking of northern Europe somewhere between the 1100s and 1500s. As royal courts embraced Christmas as the central festivity of the year, so the customs spread outward throughout society, albeit celebrated somewhat more frugally among the peasantry.

Monarchs' courts—replete with costumed jesters, entertainers, and musicians—would provide lavish spectacles, sometimes lasting the full twelve days of the season. Courtiers, often thousands of them, would be supplied with enormous quantities of food and drink to accompany the revelries. England's king Richard II was said to have employed three hundred

RIGHT: A medieval Christmas feast, as imagined by Birket Foster, 1872. The festival became a royal highlight and saw spectacles of lavish indulgence.

cooks for his Christmas banquets in the 1390s, preparing up to twenty-eight oxen and three-hundred sheep on each day of the festivities, among numerous other dishes, just to keep the supply going. Certainly, many of the conventions from the medieval period, with the various historical threads of Christmas and Yule now bound together, would persist for years, and some still remain. The dressing of houses (and churches) with greenery is something that became popular in these years, a practice that has gradually evolved into the extravaganzas people put up today. Christmas trees, in the popular form we recognize today, were still to come (see page 86), but the medieval fascination with sacred plants was extensive and would eventually lead to the later tradition's evolution. Holly, for instance, was said to ward off evil spirits, its spikes providing sharp disincentives to any invading presences.

Holly & Ivy

The carol "The Holly and the Ivy," the words of which started to appear in the early 1800s, solidifies the Christian connotations of these plants, with the holly representing Christ's crown of thorns and the ivy representing the Virgin Mary. But in medieval Europe, holly and ivy, along with other evergreens (often rosemary), were seen as especially sacred, or at least they were signs of good luck long before the famous carol came along.

As vegetation that was boldly flourishing in the cold, dark time of the year, when so much else was stark and dormant, this kind of foliage, when brought into the home, offered hope to the winter weary in the Northern Hemisphere. It reminded people that if nature could push through the harsh times and thrive again, so could they. In another echo back to Roman times, when wreaths were used as signs of victory and status, the plants would often be fashioned into circles by medieval families, decorated, and hung on doors or laid on tables.

RIGHT: Holly, with its distinctive red berries, is one of the most attractive plants to see in the cold, dark months. Its sharp leaves were once thought to help keep away evil spirits.

FAR RIGHT: Ivy, like mistletoe, is a parasitic plant that grows on trees. It has long been used to decorate homes at midwinter.

One superstition has survived from this custom. If you have ever wondered why people believe that Christmas decorations must be taken down on or by Twelfth Night (although a few hardcore Christian traditionalists extend this until Candlemas on February 2), some say it is because country folk believed the greenery was full of invisible elementals, such as elves and sprites. A truce between humans and the otherworldly visitors was in place throughout Christmastide, so all was well, but the peace ended as the season did—meaning that if you didn't get those mischievous spirits out of the house by then, they would be stuck inside all year, creating havoc and bringing bad luck. Remember this as the hanging tinsel gathers dust long after the festivities have ceased and neighbors become irritated by your lights still defiantly shining. All good things must come to an end—until next December, of course.

Candlemas

Held on February 2, this Christian feast day celebrates the moment (recorded in the Bible's Gospel of Luke) when Mary and Joseph presented Jesus at the temple in Jerusalem—a Jewish tradition that traditionally took place forty days after a baby's birth. While there, the elders Simeon and Anna are said to have recognized Jesus's importance, stating that his presence would bring redemption to the world. Candlemas has also been linked to the Celtic festival Imbolc and Roman festival Lupercalia.

Mistletoe & Wine

Other plants perceived as having magical properties also became part of seasonal folklore. The parasitic but beautiful mistletoe was used by ancient druids (the Celtic elders, recorded from around 400 BCE) to cure infertility and poisonings, while the Norse god Balder was said to have been killed by an arrow fashioned from mistletoe wood. To make up for this, according to one legend, it was only used afterward as a symbol of peace and friendship.

Mistletoe's connection to fertility is probably what would lead to the custom of kissing beneath it. The internet is awash with various explanations of where the tradition came from, but many are apocryphal. A good fact to keep in mind while navigating these theories is that, for all the oft-repeated claims of it being

Norse, Greek, or Roman in origin, this romantic little practice is not documented until the late 1700s—in England.

Norway's King Haakon may have ordered that ale must be drunk at Christmas (see page 45), but, by medieval times, another alcoholic drink was becoming associated with the season: wine, warmed with fruit and spices in a delicious concoction described as mulled. Once again, the Romans seem to be the originators of the general idea, but the first specific instruction for mulled wine in a recognizable form appears in an English recipe book (a scroll, in fact) from 1390 titled *The Forme of Cury* ("cury" derives from the French *cuire*, meaning "to cook"). Soon, no festive winter gathering would seem complete without its deeply evocative aroma.

Over time, mulled wine—and sometimes hard cider—would evolve into many equivalents, such as *glühwein* (German for "glow wine," from the heated irons used to warm it) or the Nordic *glögg*. Its calorific value would gradually increase as the sugar trade, fuelled by the horrors of the slave trade, began to give the West its sweet tooth in the seventeenth and eighteenth centuries. The mulling became ever-more adventurous as new and inventive combinations of syrups, liquors, and spices evolved.

"Here We Come a-Wassailing"

One British medieval Christmas custom still carried out in its original form in some villages today, and echoed in traditions around the world, particularly in Europe, is wassailing. Many people perform a version of it without realizing.

In an era when much of the population would often struggle to get through the harsh midwinter days, with both work and food sparse, one way of receiving charity was to go from door to door on Twelfth Night touting a bowl of hot spiced punch, usually a form of mulled cider. The bowl, often made of white maple wood, would be offered with the words *"waes hael"* or *"ves heill"*—Anglo-Saxon for "be in good health"—and the receiver would then say *"drinc hael"* ("drink hail") as they took the bowl. They would then give a gift of food or coins to the wassailer in return. In time, this greeting would also become a toast, so when people chink their glasses together and say "your health," they are, in essence, wassailing.

Other versions of wassailing include the Jaslickári troupes in Slovakia, who dress as shepherds and angels and visit homes to sing and perform, and the Koliada celebrations in Slavic nations (and also Greece), where children go from house to house in a similar fashion, receiving gifts and candies in return. Beyond being a bit of seasonal fun, which anticipated the later door-to-door activity of carol singing, wassailing was also a way of the peasantry collecting

Wassailing variations

Variations of wassailing occur on New Year's Day across the UK. Mari Lywd (meaning "the gray mare") is a Welsh custom that involves the arrival at locals' doors of a group of wassailers bearing a slightly frightening hobby horse made from a real horse's skull. The wassailers then challenge the occupants to a bizarre singing contest. The largely Scottish tradition of First Foot involves attracting the right kind of person to one's house as the first visitor of the year: preferably, a dark-haired male, carrying a piece of shortbread, a piece of coal, some salt, some black bun (a pastry-covered fruitcake), and a dram of whiskey.

RIGHT: A Carol for a Wassail Bowl, an image from the 1840s showing wassailing in an earlier time; it was a way of earning money at Christmas without having to beg.

much-needed alms from the local lords without being condemned for begging. As the old song "Here We Come a-Wassailing" puts it:

> *We are not daily beggars that beg from door to door,*
> *But we are friendly neighbors whom you have seen before.*

Some wassailers could be coercive and almost threatening in their demands for an exchange. Merry hooligans would sing rowdy songs and cast curses or damage property if their wishes weren't met. Another old song, "We Wish You a Merry Christmas," appears to commemorate this, with its demands for "figgy pudding" and the rather belligerent assertion that "We won't go till we've got some."

A variation (one of several) on the doorstep wassailing is practiced in some of the cider-producing counties of southwest England, where songs are sung in orchards and the bowl is offered to the apple trees to ward off evil spirits and ensure a good crop during the following harvest. A wassailing king and queen are often appointed to lead the ceremonies, with traditional English Morris dancers never far away.

The Feast of Stephen
(Boxing Day)

Wassailing showed that, for those with very little, it was sometimes wise to dress up a social necessity as seasonal entertainment. In time, landowners or employers across Europe would extend this principle to a more formal method of donation that would see servants, working tenants, or indeed anyone who had performed services for them throughout the year being rewarded with monetary gifts each Christmas, usually on December 26— St. Stephen's Day. (As the earliest Christian martyr, Stephen was accorded the privilege of having the first feast after Christmas Day, although he is celebrated on December 27 in the Eastern Orthodox Church.)

The charitable aspect of December 26 is remembered in the 1853 carol "Good King Wenceslas," which records the titular king's concerns on seeing a poor man in the snow "on the Feast of Stephen." He and his page retrieve the wretch from peril and provide him with meat, wine, and pine logs, setting an example to all: "Ye who now will bless the poor, shall yourselves find blessing." Wenceslas really did exist, not as a king but as a Duke of Bohemia (now in the modern Czech Republic) in the 900s; he had a reputation for wisdom and kindness—although this did not stop him from eventually being murdered on the orders of his brother. His piety was rewarded, in the afterlife at least, by being declared a saint shortly after his death.

December 26 became known in Great Britain and some of its colonies as "Boxing Day," seemingly with a number of origins. The early Christian custom of metal boxes being placed outside churches to collect coins on St. Stephen's Day is

LEFT: The poor man in the snow meets the page of Good King Wenceslas, seen here from an 1879 book by Henry Ramsden Bramley.

one reason, while another is the tradition where apprentices displayed earthenware boxes into which masters or customers dropped tips over Christmastide. The boxes were broken open when full. More generally, money was collected in boxes throughout the year by nobles and institutions to be distributed as alms at this time. Other boxes included those sometimes given to privileged servants who were given time off the day after Christmas (which they would have spent working, of course) containing bonuses, presents, and leftover food for their families.

By the 1700s, however, the growing expectation that cash gifts (by then known generically as boxes, even if a box wasn't involved) must be given to anyone who had performed the slightest task for the giver was beginning to seed resentment. With the number of beneficiaries growing each year, in 1710 the author Jonathan Swift wrote, "By the lord Harry I shall be undone here with Christmas boxes." As a result, this altruistic element of the season would be gradually watered down and Boxing Day would evolve into an opportunity for recovery after all the excess, or for people today, a repeat of Christmas but with a different set of relatives. For others, it has become an opportunity for sporting fixtures; British aristocrats, for instance, traditionally meet for fox hunts, although now only for the pageantry, and in Australia special cricket tournaments and yacht races take place.

In some countries, St. Stephen's Day is a time for curious folk rituals such as Wren Day in Ireland (in which wrens, once real but now happily fake, are pursued), or stoning in some of the Germanic countries, a drinking activity that involves young men leaving church and then, perhaps paradoxically, drinking as much as possible afterward. Don't necessarily expect to celebrate Boxing Day in the United States, as many people return to work that day, although it is a national holiday in Canada. Revelers in the Bahamas, meanwhile, enjoy the festival of Junkanoo on this day, with street parades, much dancing, and beautifully elaborate costumes.

Holming

One tradition that no longer exists on this day is the Welsh custom of holming, which involved beating female servants and late risers with holly branches. It allegedly brought good luck, but for whom is not clear!

Gift Giving

Christmastide has traditionally been seen as a time of giving as well as receiving, as the traditions of distributing alms testify; a chance to think of the needs of others even as we treat ourselves. This has long expressed itself in people buying nice things for the ones they love.

In keeping with the earlier Roman custom, giving gifts was at first more associated with the time around New Year than with Christmas. These gifts were perhaps not what one would imagine today, and their nature depended on one's class. In Tudor times, the English monarch would often donate gold or silver to their favorites (one year, Elizabeth I gave 136 ounces of plate to Earl Robert Dudley, while the court dwarf received 2 ounces); the recipients would, if possible, reciprocate with their own generous, or at least well-meant, gifts—that is, if they wanted to remain favorites. This custom is echoed today, in one direction at least, in the British royal New Year's Honours lists.

As pagan influences gave way to a Christian context, gift giving moved to Christmas time, perhaps inspired by the gifts brought to Jesus by the wise men. It was middle-class Victorians who began the arms race of beautifully wrapped and often expensive gifts piled under the tree.

If all of this sounds relatively modest compared to the extravaganzas of today, you can partly thank nineteenth-century New Yorkers for the change. While Christmas was frowned upon by Puritan settlers (more on that in the next chapter), by the 1800s, public celebrations in the streets of America were a seasonal tradition. This was fun for the poorer celebrants, who were free to enjoy a time of misrule (see page 60), but because New York's population increased tenfold between 1800 and 1850, wealthier New Yorkers started to worry that street parties might become riots. Hence, the upper echelons promoted the idea of a domestic Christmas instead, with gift exchanges at

Different days of giving

Not all countries choose Christmas Day for giving gifts. A number of European countries swap gifts on Christmas Eve. The Russian Orthodox Church calendar celebrates Christmas on January 7, and most Russians exchange gifts at New Year. These, legend has it, are brought by the blue-robed Grandfather Frost and his granddaughter Snegurochka the Snow Maiden.

home. Middle-class families, happy to keep their children away from what they saw as rowdy influences, quickly adopted the idea. By 1867, shopping for toys had become big enough business that New York's flagship Macy's store began remaining open until midnight on Christmas Eve. With postwar America setting much of the world's Christmas tone (see page 127), domestic gift giving became the order of the day in most countries that celebrated the festival.

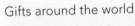

LEFT: By the twentieth century, the giving of seasonal gifts was generating entire industries. Here, customers at New York's R. H. Macy & Co. carry out their Christmas shopping.

Gifts around the world

LEBANON: Children enjoy a particular right when it comes to gifts. On Christmas Day, they can approach any adult and say, *"Editi aleik!"* (You have a present for me). If they've picked an adult who has a suitable gift on hand, they give it to the child.

SYRIA: Legend has it that gifts for children are brought by camel—specifically, the youngest camel from the Magi's train, who, according to the tale, collapsed exhausted after the long journey.

ICELAND: This country enjoys the peaceful practice of giving books on December 24. The custom is so widespread that publishers refer to the Jólabókaflóð, or Christmas book flood. Families exchange books and, traditionally, curl up with hot chocolate to settle in and read away the evening.

The Rule of Misrule

Despite the emphasis placed today on gifts and greetings, for the Europeans of the medieval times, there was a seasonal focus that meant far more to them—letting go of all trouble and strife and giving into what was known as misrule.

When people get drunk and disorderly at Christmas today, there is a general air of disapproval from observers who do not join in, or bleak headlines in the papers with photos of young men and women staggering in streets and rolling in gutters. In earlier centuries, however, people would have thought they weren't celebrating

correctly if they *weren't* getting merrily out of hand. For all the church-going and religious devotion of the time, such disorder was not seen as contradictory, and thus became formalized in ways that can seem surprising compared to our generally more contained ways of observance today (perhaps with the exception of the odd riotous office Christmas party).

Misrule's somewhat anarchic expression in wild games and forfeits, practical jokes, singing and dancing, plenty of drinking, and the many different forms of wassailing turned things on their head and helped people through the dark winter. Twelve days of wild fun, happily dictated by the cycle set down centuries before, served to bring everyone's year full circle, allowing for a brief respite before getting ready for another hardworking year ahead. Once the hangovers had cleared, anyway.

These Christmastide traditions of misrule seem to echo back, by coincidence or direct lineage, to the Roman Saturnalia festivities (see page 17), but the growth of seasonal misrule also, surprisingly, had its origins in the Church. From around the twelfth century, a European custom arose, first in France, whereby young trainee clergy were appointed as Boy Bishops and given special dispensation at Christmas to carry out more adult ecclesiastical duties, such as giving blessings and performing ceremonies, but also, conversely, to enjoy and lead the Feast of Fools. This was a form of partying that saw burlesques acted out for their own entertainment and pranks being played on one another. It built to such a level of perceived disgrace by the higher clergy that, by the mid-1300s, there were not entirely successful attempts by archbishops to stamp it out. The tradition survived, however. Boy Bishops were elected on December 6, the feast of the children's patron St. Nicholas, and ruled until December 28 (The Feast of the Holy Innocents, commemorating King Herod's killing of the firstborn in the Nativity story).

As misrule leaked into the wider community, some Tudor schools began to adopt their own routines of entertaining defiance, such as "barring out," an extraordinary Christmastide practice that saw schoolboys barricading themselves into the main classroom. If they could hold out for more than three days, masters would grant concessions to pupil's demands, but if the barricades were broken down, the pupils would be flogged. People's ways of entertaining themselves were clearly very different back then.

Despite several further attempts to ban the custom, misrule became rife throughout European society, and the role of Boy Bishop had, by the 1500s, evolved into the broader societal figure of the Lord of Misrule or Abbott of Unreason (in themselves throwbacks to Saturnalia's mock kings). It would be a member of the community elected or compelled to direct riotous high jinks and come up with the games, silly plays, and imaginative forfeits that would distract everyone from their hard and often dull lives. This largely drunken haze would last just long enough to see revelers through to Epiphany and the inevitable return to harsh reality (although luxuriating nobles would join in happily, too, as evidenced by surviving records of expenses spent on misrule events). By comparison, a game of Scrabble over turkey sandwiches seems quite tame.

RIGHT: Christmas misrule would often involve wearing grotesque costumes and masks, as the merry revelers sought to subvert everyday normality.

CHAPTER THREE

CHRISTMAS UNDER THREAT

Christmas Under Threat

In 1527, King Henry VIII of England decided to seek an annulment of his marriage so he could marry his new love Anne Boleyn, and Pope Clement VII refused to grant it. The stage was set for a struggle that would see Henry setting up his own Protestant Church of England with the monarchy in charge. This occurred even as a general reform movement swept across parts of Europe, courtesy of devout agitators, such as Germany's Martin Luther. The Reformation questioned many former doctrinal certainties, advocated previously banned vernacular Bibles, and stripped away both assets and physical church architecture. It saw huge changes across Europe and the destruction of Catholic institutions in England, creating international divides that would shape the next few centuries through war and social strife. One result of all this turmoil was that Christmas would also find itself under threat.

The new English Church continued under Henry's nine-year-old son Edward VI in 1547, but when Edward himself died just six years later, his half-sister Mary I promptly returned the nation to Catholicism, executing the very last court-appointed Lord of

LEFT: As part of Henry VIII's English Reformation, Catholic nuns and monks were expelled from convents, monasteries and abbeys.

Misrule, George Ferrers, together with hundreds of Protestant martyrs. When Henry's daughter Elizabeth I acceded in 1558, she restored most of the Protestant reforms, outraging the remaining Catholic countries. But a number of hardcore campaigners did not believe she had gone far enough. Now seeing Catholicism, or popery, as heresy—a tyrannical foreign influence riddled with corruption, arcane rituals, and iconographic distractions from true faith—a growing movement, with influence in Parliament, called for a full purification of the new Church. Its proponents became collectively known as Puritans, and to them, any Holy Days not directly specified or dated in the Bible (in other words, all but the Sabbath) were sacrilegious. The now huge edifice of Christmas was the worst offender in this regard.

For nations securely under Catholic or Orthodox control, Christmas and other liturgical and folk traditions continued, and even in other Protestant nations the fight was less fierce. Martin Luther himself, for instance, loved Christmas and preached numerous sermons on its meaning. But English Puritanism had a disproportionate influence; although they didn't know it at the time, the Puritans would eventually become the founders of what would become the United States of America, a superpower that would help reshape Christmas for the entire world. Before this, however, they were very much against the festival.

Many Puritans reasoned that—with its origins indelibly mixed with solstice rituals from unenlightened times and its evolution having emphasized the misrule element above the message of Christ—Christmas was now simply an annual invitation to drunkenness and sin. Presbyterians, following the example of the Swiss Calvinists (a strict and influential Protestant movement), believed this strongly and took the bold step of banning Christmas in Scotland as early as 1583. Aside from a brief attempt by James I to resuscitate the Scottish celebrations in 1617, and other occasional resistances, incredibly, the ban was officially lifted only in 1958. This didn't mean Christmas had not revived there by then, but it was never the big event that it was south of the border. The Scots simply transferred misrule and feasting to the New Year Hogmanay festivities, and, eventually, Burns Night (celebrating the popular Ayrshire poet Robert Burns) on January 25—which neatly demonstrates that when you take away something that people want, they will only re-create it. But English reformers were eager to follow the Scots' example. The Puritan attitude toward

Christmas is summed up in Philip Stubbes's tellingly titled diatribe *The Anatomie of Abuses*, published the same year as the Presbyterians' ban:

> *More mischief is that time committed than in all the year besides; what masking and mumming, whereby robbery, whoredom, murder and what not is committed? What dicing and carding, what eating and drinking, what banqueting and feasting is then used, more than in all the year besides, to the great dishonour of God and impoverishing of the realm.*

Christmas was in trouble.

Mummers

Stubbes's "mumming" refers to a tradition in Great Britain whereby costumed actors and entertainers known as mummers burst into homes unannounced and entertained the occupants until they gave a gift or donation. Often, it would be men dressed as women (known as Mollies or Bessies), and, occasionally, women dressed as men—the exact kinds of perceived immoralities the Puritans despised. These traditions still live on in British theaters in the guise of pantomimes, anarchic comedies performed during the Christmas period; they are one of the last vestiges of organized misrule.

The End of Christmas

ABOVE: This illustration by Howard Pyle ca. 1883, of a Puritan governor stopping Christmas sports, sums up the mood of the seasonal suppression.

Christmas might have remained safe had the Puritans remained a minority movement, but their influence grew in England when, in the 1600s, a dispute arose between King Charles I and his own Parliament over a number of religious and political issues. From 1642, the country found itself embroiled in the English Civil War, although this series of conflicts, which unfolded over several years, actually encompassed England, Scotland, and Ireland, creating bitter divisions. When Puritan general, Oliver Cromwell, finally led Parliament to victory over the monarchy, Great Britain was left at the mercy of a Puritan-led republic that could do anything it wanted—and one of the first things it wanted to do was ban Christmas. Banning Christmas is not a uniquely English phenomenon—China, Russia, North Korea, Saudi Arabia, and Somalia are just some of the nations that have attempted to stamp it out at one time or another, even in modern times, for religious or political reasons. However, England was one of the first and went further than most.

In 1647, with Charles I now in captivity, Christmas was officially banned by a decree of Parliament after a buildup of general suppression. This draconian move might seem astonishing today, but such was the religious fervor then gripping the reins of power. Because Christmas was no longer a Holy Day, churches were ordered to cease their services in all British territories—although some at first refused—and all civic merriments ended.

This prohibition applied to England and its colonies, especially in the new North America. The Pilgrim Fathers were, after all, Puritans and had already thrown out Christmas; although the Plymouth Rock landings took place around December 1620 and the settlers had plenty of hardships to keep them busy, they refused to lighten the gloom by celebrating their first Christmas Day in the New World. On the contrary, they made a point of working in the fields as if there was nothing special about the day. Gift giving at Christmas didn't even become legal until the 1680s—although it is notable that Americans quickly created a Thanksgiving festival in November, giving them a winter celebration that did not offend their doctrine.

LEFT: Puritan family meals were austere, but still sometimes celebratory. With Christmas shunned by early American settlers, Thanksgiving filled the gap.

In the more disputatious British Isles, the banning of Christmastide was far from popular. There were immediate challenges from those whose favorite time of the year had been so savagely pulled from the schedule. After years of civil war and growing hostility toward the new Puritan republic over high taxation and the maintenance of its huge armies, along with a burgeoning of repressive policies (public singing and dancing were heavily frowned upon), the seasonal prohibition tipped many people over the edge. Riots broke out in a number of cities and developed into general pro-Royalist protests, most notably in Ipswich, where one rioter was killed. In Canterbury, mobs smashed stores that refused to close for Christmas and events threatened to escalate into full-scale insurrection.

The Vindication of Christmas

Christmas in seventeenth-century England was fast becoming something celebrated in secret, and even that became dangerous. Defiant displays of holly and ivy at places such as St. Margaret's church in Westminster and the public water conduit in London's Cornhill were torn down by the authorities and the perpetrators arrested. Tales were told, fictitious or not, of soldiers roaming the streets listening for carols being sung and smelling the air for seasonal food being cooked. Certainly, Scotland did see such intimidation in its own earlier ban, when a local minister, Murdoch Mackenzie, roamed the glens, rifling through kitchens seeking any sign of the Christmas goose being prepared, warning suspects that its feathers "would rise up in judgment against them one day."

People not turning up for work and stores mysteriously failing to open (often many of them), were other probable indications of surreptitious festivity. If found out, fines were imposed on revelers, occasionally even imprisonment. The anti-Christmas enforcement, however, was reportedly half-hearted; even some of the soldiers were noted to question it, while the House of Commons itself tended to be oddly ill-attended on December 25.

By the 1650s, with Charles I beheaded and Oliver Cromwell governing the nation as Lord Protector, the spirit of the season seemed at last to have been crushed in England and its territories, with most churches remaining closed and few people daring to show open signs of celebration. Christmas was finally dead.

Or was it? In truth, the abolition of Christmas had never truly been solid and rumblings and quiet resistance were present from the beginning. Even in the run-up to the scrapping of Christmas, some scholars had publicly argued for its continuation. One such was the clergyman Edward Fisher's influential *Feast of Feasts*. First published in 1644, it was pointedly reissued in 1649, two years into the Christmas ban. The 1649 issue of this publication was retitled *A Christian Caveat to the Old and New Sabbatarians*. Fisher argued that Christmas should be allowed on the technicality that scriptural analysis made it clear to him that "the 25th day of December is the just, true, and exact day of our Savior's birth." Proving this position was another matter and he was not widely supported in his beliefs, but his pro-Christmas stance certainly anticipated the mood of future times.

Pamphleteering wasn't limited to scholars. For the more populist market, there were lively satires, such as John Taylor's *The Complaint of Christmas* (1631), which imagined Father Christmas (an early version of Santa Claus) arriving to little welcome in a bleak London, where a crowd complains: "Thus are the merry lords of misrule suppressed by the mad lords of bad rule at Westminster." The mischievous *The Arraignment, Conviction and Imprisoning of Christmas* (1646) claimed its printer was one "Simon Minc'd-Pie for Cissely Plum-porridge," demonstrating its tongue-in-cheek approach and disdain for the Puritan hostility to humor and fun.

As the years of Puritan rule began to grate, the distribution of openly pro-Christmas publications grew. Taylor's sequel to *The Complaint of Christmas*, for instance, was published in 1653, and entitled *The Vindication of Christmas* (1653). Such pamphlets stirred further feelings, even as people stirred secret seasonal dishes. How long could this untenable situation really last? By the middle of the 1650s, with Cromwell now an increasingly unwell and isolated dictator of a much-resented fundamentalist state, the cracks in both its power and the Christmas ban were beginning to show.

The diarist John Evelyn records wanting to attend a London Christmas Day church service in both 1652 and 1655 and failing to find one but, by 1657, significantly, he was able to locate a "grand assembly" at Exeter House chapel in the Strand. He and other attendees were arrested and questioned before being released, but the fact that at least two other services took place in London that day makes clear that the public was sensing change and increasingly prepared to take risks.

It took the passing of Cromwell for the dam to burst. Indeed, while he lay dying in the early days of September 1658, a wild, damaging storm hit England and was seen by those who believed in portents as God's judgment on the nation. The republic briefly passed to his son Richard, but he lacked the same leadership qualities and civil restlessness set in. The remains of the government, after all the years of strife to remove the monarchy, realized that only by reviving it would stability be maintained. Thus, with huge ceremony and not a little irony, Charles II (son of the dead king) was finally installed in May 1660. With this Restoration came the hope that Christmas might also be restored.

Philanthropic pamphleteers

While a love of Christmas merriment motivated the satirical pamphleteers, some campaigners also argued the case for Christmas on a humanitarian basis, pointing out the importance of the charitable nature of Christmas in hard times. In a 1647 book entitled *A Ha! Christmas*, a mysterious T.H. wrote:

At such time as Christmas, those who God Almighty hath given a good share of the wealth of this world, may wear the best, eat and drink the best with moderation, so that they remember Christ's poor members with mercy and charity....

Whether silly or solemn, Christmas defenders were on the rise.

CHAPTER FOUR

THE SEASON'S RETURN

The Season's Return

Keen to put distance between his new reign and the drab Puritan years, Charles II, being in any case something of a playboy (begetting twelve illegitimate children) who relished naughtiness and gaiety, reinstated much that the hardline Protestants had taken away—and rebooting Christmas was perhaps his most symbolic act. His quiet sympathies with the old Catholic ways would become a problem in time, but many people were happy to re-embrace the old feast days with gusto.

Much of England breathed a sigh of relief as the old years of repression began to fall away. The famous diarist, Samuel Pepys, recorded attending a church decorated with "rosemary and baize" (bay) on December 23, 1660, before returning home to a great turkey. Sumptuous meals could now be eaten without fear of retribution.

Ultimately, the enforced austerity of the Puritans was the very thing that undid them, breeding resentment. Removed from power, their influence would quickly fade. Celebrating is a natural impulse; attempting to take that away seemed antilife, whatever the rightness of their belief that the Church had become bloated and corrupt. The fact that even some Puritan ministers were holding Christmas Day services again by 1662 speaks volumes.

The times had changed, and Christmas in England was back—although it would take a while to return to full strength. While the colonies officially legalized Christmas in 1681, for many decades the holiday was simply unimportant to most citizens, especially those in the areas founded by Puritans. The famous Massachusetts Puritan preacher,

RIGHT: An elaborate Christmas masque (show) is performed for King Charles II, as depicted in the nineteenth-century *London Illustrated News*.

Cotton Mather, for instance, had inveighed against the holiday's "rude reveling" and "Saturnalian jollities." In less straitlaced states, however, the influence of settlers from other cultures was leading to a more relaxed attitude. In Philadelphia, Benjamin Franklin, for instance, described matters in the 1739 edition of *Poor Richard's Almanac*:

Puritan Christmas

Once Christmas returned, even Puritans got into the spirit. On Christmas Day 1667, English Puritan minister Ralph Josselin wrote in his diary, "Preached and feasted my tenants and all my children with joy. Lord sanctify."

> *O blessed Season! Lov'd by Saints and Sinners,*
> *For long Devotions, or for longer Dinners*

Official recognition trickled in state by state, starting with Alabama declaring it a public holiday in 1836, but only in 1870 was Christmas declared a federal holiday. The United States was slow to catch onto Christmas, but once it did, it embraced it with lavish enthusiasm.

Christmas Carols

The word "carol" may derive either from the Old French/Middle English *carole* ("to dance"), or the Latin *choraula* ("a choral song") or *carula* ("a circular dance"). The first records of seasonal choral music, then serious and sung in Latin, can be traced to fourth-century Roman Christians. By the ninth century, these had evolved into sequences sung in monasteries, which themselves then turned into rhyming stanzas. It took a twelfth-century French monk, Adam of St. Victor, to start to blend Christmas words with well-known folk tunes. With the help of people such as St. Francis of Assisi, who used them in his nativity plays in the early 1200s, their popularity grew. By the 1400s, there were at least twenty-five recognized carols sung by wassailers on street doorsteps, although some had little in common with the Christian Nativity and more to do with misrule and jollity (see page 60).

English-language carols suffered something of a rebuff under Puritan rule, but it is difficult to stamp out folk music and, with a little refinement, many carols gradually found their way back into churches across Europe as an accepted part of Christmas worship. Their long development means it is sometimes hard to trace their exact origins, but early versions (still in Latin) of at least some of them can be found as early as 1582 in the collection *Piae Cantiones*, which includes "Good King Wenceslas" and "Good Christian Men, Rejoice." This volume held great cultural significance. Schooling in the era was almost entirely under the control of the Church, and singing was part of the pupils' curriculum; such volumes became known to every educated person. *Piae Cantiones* include songs that originated from Germany, Austria, Czechoslovakia, Poland, Finland, Switzerland, Spain, England, Italy, and France, dating from the thirteenth to fifteenth centuries, making it a cultural treasure trove—and because poorer student singers would perform in the

A UNESCO carol

Perhaps the most truly global Christmas carol is "Stille Nacht" (Silent Night). First sung on Christmas Eve 1818, in Obendorf, Austria, with lyrics by priest Joseph Mohr and music by organist Franz Gruber, this haunting carol has been translated into more than 300 languages. In 2011, UNESCO added the song to its Intangible Cultural Heritage list in tribute to its international status.

streets to help raise money for their school fees, the carols formed a link between social classes as well as nations.

The influence of carol books continued to be felt. Carols were hugely popular in the nineteenth century, and a major contributor was the publication of *Christmas Carols Ancient and Modern* in 1833, with words and music edited and arranged by William B. Sandys, partly inspired by Davies Gilbert's 1823 work *Some Ancient Christmas Carols*. Sandys's collection gathered together a rich trove of carols from previously disparate and remote sources, sharing with the world such songs as "The First Nowell," "I Saw Three Ships," and "God Rest Ye Merry Gentlemen," which might otherwise have languished in obscurity.

Carols around the world

FRANCE: "Petit Papa Noel" ("Little Father Christmas"). A child sings an appeal to Father Christmas not to forget *"mon petit soulier"* ("my little shoe"), then suggests he wraps up warm in the cold, ruefully admitting that Father Christmas being out there is *"un peu à cause de moi"* ("a little bit because of me").

ITALY: "Caro Gesù Bambino" ("Dear Baby Jesus"). Another song sung by a child, who invites the infant Jesus to descend from the sky and *"vieni a giocar"* ("come play").

THE PHILIPPINES: "Ang Paso Ay Sumapit" ("Christmas Has Arrived"). A bouncy tune that celebrates love and pledges all-year-round sharing.

PORTUGAL: "O Menino Está Dormindo" ("The Boy Is Sleeping"). A simple carol describing the resting baby in the arms of the Virgin.

RUSSIA: "The Forest Raised a Christmas Tree." This tells of a tree's growth (during which it sheltered a rabbit from a hungry wolf), before being felled and decorated for a party.

Shepherds & Partridges

When first transcribed in 1696, Irish poet Nahum Tate's "While Shepherds Watched Their Flocks by Night," which faithfully records Luke's account of the Nativity, was the one and only Christmas hymn permitted by the Anglican Church. It was a time when only words derived directly from Scripture were seen as acceptable—a hangover from Puritan rule. This may explain why there is an unusually high number of different tunes for the carol beyond those explained by the usual regional rearrangements. People listening to carol singers (who naturally developed from wassailers) might have become resentful of the same tune being sung at them over and over again, but even if the words couldn't change, the notes could.

In time, Christmas songs flourished and became more adventurous. First emerging in the mid-1700s, for instance, the traditional "The Twelve Days of Christmas" would become a favorite in a number of countries. This entertaining if absurd cycle of verses, with all its maids-a-milking, lords-a-leaping, and an incongruous partridge in a pear tree, seems on the surface, to have arisen from a word-memory game, probably played on Twelfth Night to great hilarity, with forfeits paid for mistakes. In France, a plainly related cumulative verse became known as "Les Douze Mois" ("The Twelve Months"), or

Colly or calling?

If you have ever sung, as many do, "four colly birds" and have been corrected by someone that you should be singing "four *calling* birds" instead, vindication may yet be yours. The words of a version from 1780 clearly have it as "colly birds"—"colly" once meaning "black" in some parts of England. There were all kinds of spelling variations of this line, in fact, until the 1909 Frederic Austin version (which also introduced the "five gold rings" melodic variation) finally standardized it as "calling," thus setting up family conflicts over the Christmas table for years to come.

Behind the lyrics

Could the twelve days of Christmas secretly embody Roman Catholic beliefs, as compiled during the years of their repression? Some people believe so and interpret the meaning of the song as listed here:

A partridge in a pear tree = Jesus Christ

Two turtle doves = the Old and New Testaments

Three French hens = the Holy Trinity

Four calling (colly) birds = the Bible's four gospels or evangelists

Five gold rings = the first five Old Testament books

Six geese a-laying = the six days of creation

Seven swans a-swimming = the seven sacraments of the Catholic Church

Eight maids a-milking = the eight Beatitudes

Nine ladies dancing = the nine fruits of the Holy Spirit

Ten lords a-leaping = the Ten Commandments

Eleven pipers piping = Jesus's eleven faithful apostles

Twelve drummers drumming = the twelve points of the Apostles' Creed

"La Perdriole," meaning "The Partridge." As years passed and different versions of the song merged, the themes progressively spiraled and mutated (peculiarly, in some parts of northern England the song had only ten days of Christmas for a while) and tunes came and went until finally settling into the version people know and love, or are irritated by, today.

Some scholars have suggested that at least some of the words of "The Twelve Days of Christmas" may even be allegorical representations of Christian beliefs, particularly Roman Catholic ones, formulated during eras where expressing them in song was prohibited or frowned upon. It is a controversial view, but one that continues to generate debate.

The Slow Recovery
of Christmas

One of the great ironies of the Puritan ban on Christmas was that it encouraged the creation of more secular forms of celebration around the solstice as surreptitious replacements. These were closer to the original pre-Christian customs, as we have seen with the Scottish elevation of Hogmanay (see page 65) and, eventually, Burns Night, which would see carols replaced by the likes of "Auld Lang Syne," with words by Burns that roughly translate as "for the sake of old times." Even today, evangelical leaflets exclaiming "We're putting Christ back into Christmas" flourish every December, decrying the loss of the Christian message. Yet the unavoidable truth is that (Protestant) Christianity took Christ out of Christmas in the first place by wiping out the Holy Days and, after this, the religious elements of the festival never returned to their previous level.

When you remove a celebration, you create a vacuum. In countries affected by bans, more pagan elements of Yule and other winter festivals tended to creep back in. In other cases, the festivities were secularized and moved to a different date, such as when the Soviet Union rebranded Christmas as a New Year celebration in 1935—or when Americans created a lavish Thanksgiving feasting day in November, conveniently close to winter.

Although Christmas was officially reinstated across British territories after 1660, broader social changes were brewing, ones that would slow down its full revival.

By the late 1700s, the Industrial Revolution had begun in Europe. Machine-orientated factories sprung up and people migrated from the country in large numbers to work in crowded cities under low black clouds. Many of the old Christmas traditions were rooted in rural life, and although people did their best to maintain them in new conditions, the reality was that it was hard to keep the same spirit alive. With furnaces that needed to be kept burning, and

RIGHT: The Industrial Revolution in Europe threatened Christmas traditions, which were hard to maintain in cities governed by factory life and economic demands.

money to be kept rolling in, factory owners were hardly inclined to honor the several days of holiday that country dwellers had come to expect. Before long, workers were doing well to be given a single day off over Christmas. Even then, families were often scattered and fragmented, diluting the crucial togetherness that the season once engendered. What heights could misrule and merriment really rise to under such restrictions, and with no allowed recovery time?

By the eighteenth century, Great Britain held a vast and influential empire, but Christmas cheer was no longer one of its exports. An indication of this can be gauged from the fact that in twenty of the years between 1790 and 1835, *The Times*, the key British newspaper of its day, failed to mention Christmas at all on December 25, so meaningless had the festival become to most of its readers. And yet the British "Victorian Christmas" of the mid- to late nineteenth century has become an idealized nostalgic vision of the season that people still look back to in modern times. So how and why did Christmas recover during this period?

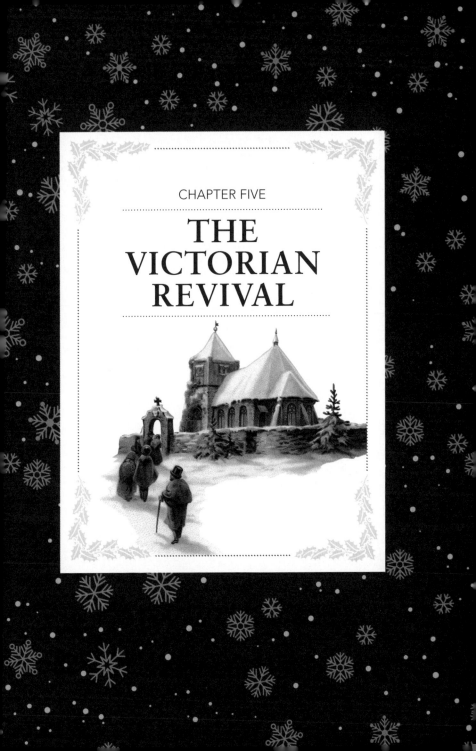

CHAPTER FIVE

THE VICTORIAN REVIVAL

The Victorian Revival

When walking around the city precincts and town squares of many Western countries in the run-up to Christmas, a curious phenomenon can become apparent. Jolly folk in top hats and coattails or fancy crinolines are often strolling, giving out leaflets, collecting for charity or singing carols, while chestnut vendors dressed in nineteenth-century outfits give the impression of having traveled through some bizarre time portal.

So why the nostalgia for Victorian celebration, as the British call it, and not any number of the multiple centuries that saw all kinds of Christmases in many guises? The Victorians themselves looked back to medieval celebrations as their own inspiration, yet reshaped them into something else altogether.

Much of the contemporary Christmas traditions have their roots in Queen Victoria of England's reign in the mid-1800s, a crucial time of revival for a festival that was falling into obscurity. New German influence from her marriage to Prince Albert would play a major role, but the Christmas revival can also be partly linked to the rise of the "Oxford movement" from around 1833—a delayed reaction against the hardline Protestant Church's rejection of religious art and ritual. These new leading Protestant thinkers saw no conflict in wanting to bring back some of the more arcane and mysterious aspects of services, such as restoring the central role of Communion and the wearing of elaborate vestments, which had been buried in the earlier anti-papist hysteria.

Reinstalling the key Holy Days at the heart of Anglican Christianity brought the concept of an annual ritual cycle celebrating saints and key events from the Gospels back into full consciousness and saw Christmas and Easter find new importance. The desire for such revival had already been demonstrated by the popularity of John Keble's influential 1827 poetry tome *The Christian Year*. Keble, along with Cardinal Newman, was a leader in the Oxford movement, and they would create the separate branch of Anglicanism known as "Anglo-Catholicism." The Oxford movement was opposed by old-school Protestants still fearing papist infiltration; a number of court cases were even launched against it, but when it came to Christmas rituals, they definitely emerged the winners.

RIGHT: A family at Christmas in Berlin, Germany, around 1900.

Prince Albert's German Christmas

Despite the influence of Protestant reformers, Christmas in Germany had retained many of its jollities. Indeed, many seasonal traditions began there, and the traditional German Christmas markets, full of gingerbread and *glühwein*, still draw tourists from across Europe today or are eagerly copied in other countries. Religious traditions had been challenged by Protestant theology, especially Puritanism, but the great Protestant reformer Martin Luther is actually credited (at least by legend) as having created the first Christmas tree (see page 88).

Before the British Victorian era, Germany was well ahead of Europe and the New World in terms of Christmas spirit. The British royal family had brought a Germanic bloodline into the line of succession with George I in 1714, but it took the arrival of the dynamic Prince Albert, to really bring German cheer to the fore. When he married Queen Victoria in 1840, Albert brought his home country's traditions with him, and thus spread the results across the burgeoning Empire.

Advent wreath

A German tradition that persists to this day is the *Adventskranz*, or Advent wreath. Evergreen branches are woven together to create a flat "crown," usually placed on a table, with four candles; one is lit every Sunday of December.

Albert's eagerness to reinstall the beloved Christmas traditions he had grown up with coincided with the rise of a new, often middle-class, social conscience. The official abolition of the slave trade in Great Britain in 1833 had raised awareness of the wicked abuses inflicted on other peoples, and it began to also draw attention to the abuses present in its own factories—especially concerning children and the plight of the poor. With society fearing civil unrest through want, the old charitable side of Christmastide thus found a new impetus.

RIGHT: German Christmas markets are imitated throughout Europe; they include stalls selling Christmas decorations, gifts, and traditional German food.

With the reawakening of the Christmas spirit, a slew of fresh or revived customs arrived to go with it, giving birth to many of the seasonal delights now taken for granted and explaining why Victorian Christmas remains as a romanticized template. By the end of the nineteenth century, the festival would be celebrated as a major event again in many countries, encapsulated by the growing success of artistic works such as Tchaikovsky's ballet *The Nutcracker*, first performed in St. Petersburg, Russia, in 1892. A much-beloved fantasy of toys coming to life one Christmas Eve, it was a clear sign the magic of the season had returned.

With both Prince Albert and Queen Victoria sharing concerns that the central role of the family was being undermined by rapid social change, there were specific attempts to remind people of the importance of the season and the potential closeness it offered. Images of blissful family life at the palace were intentionally distributed at Christmas, an impression of calm domesticity replacing the perceived seasonal excesses of previous royal courts, and implying a resonance with archetypal representations of the Holy Family.

A crude Christmas

One Spanish tradition (mainly in Catalonia) that may seem outrageous to others is the inclusion in a crib scene of a *caganer* (literally, "the defecator"). This comic squatting figure, usually a folk-costumed man with dropped pants and bare backside, began to arrive in local Nativity scenes as early as the eighteenth century for reasons not entirely clear. Some say it represents fertility (in the manure sense) or is a reminder to authority figures of the leveling nature of bodily functions. Others suspect it was just a Catalan having a disrespectful laugh one year that somehow stuck as a tradition. These days you can buy a wild variety of novelty *caganers* in Spain—squatting superheroes, cartoon characters, and celebrities all fill the gift store shelves. Continuing a theme, Catalans are also fond of the Tio de Nadal ("pooping log"), a small hollowed-out tree trunk filled with small gifts, which are encouraged out of its posterior at Christmas by hitting it with sticks.

RIGHT: Images of Queen Victoria and Prince Albert's family gathered around a glowing tree, published in the late 1840s, popularized Christmas trees.

Perhaps not coincidentally, the building of Nativity cribs in homes became more common in these times. These figurines of the Holy Family focused attention back onto the image of the family itself, in a period when the ties were often strained through the demands of factory life. Cribs eventually became the central decoration in some Christian homes. At least, that is, until Christmas trees came along.

Prince Albert is frequently credited with bringing the first Christmas tree to Great Britain, or even inventing the idea completely, but dressed trees go back many years (see page 90). Even in England, the first known royal example had already appeared at Windsor Castle courtesy of George III's wife Charlotte in 1800. In her 1832 journal, the thirteen-year-old Princess Victoria herself recorded "two trees hung with lights (candles) and sugar ornaments. All the presents being placed round the tree." So the Christmas tree was already established, but it was nonetheless about to make its true ascent.

89

Christmas Trees

Who can claim the honor of setting up the first Christmas tree? There is no clear answer. Ceremonial trees have a long lineage: ancient Turks were said to adorn "wishing trees" with ribbons for the sky god Bai-Ulgan on December 23; druids sometimes decorated trees as signs of veneration, and tree worship was known among Vikings and Saxons. Meanwhile, using evergreens for winter decorations goes back well before the Christian era, with cultures from Egypt and China to Scandinavia using fresh branches to symbolize life and safety in the dark times.

In medieval times, meanwhile, mystery plays exploring the themes behind Christianity would be performed on Christmas Eve, and one recurring story was that of Adam and Eve. To symbolize the Garden of Eden's Tree of Life, or Paradise Tree, a real or artificial tree would be dressed with apples (the forbidden fruit, representing humankind's first sin), and paper disks or wafers (the Communion host, or Eucharist, representing redemption). Perhaps it was these trees that inspired the use of blown-glass balls and other fancy decorations. Some observers have speculated that the ornamental spheres may represent the orb of the solstice sun.

> ### Weihnachtsbaum
>
> **The German for Christmas tree is not Tannenbaum, as in the popular song "O Tannenbaum," but Weihnachtsbaum. Tannenbaum simply refers to a generic fir tree.**

A good candidate for the first proper Christmas tree can be found in a German legend from the 1500s. A popular tale credits the reformer Martin Luther with the inspiration. Walking through frosty woods on Christmas Eve, he was so struck with the starlight glittering on icicle-hung tree branches that he brought one home to his family. He is also said to have been the first to light up a tree; inspired by the bright stars in the sky, he attached candles to the branches to remind them all of the heavens from where Jesus came. Even now, many trees are topped with a star or an angel (or a fairy for the more secular), making a clear link to the Nativity story.

Whether or not this really was the first occasion—the Estonian city of Tallin and the Latvian capital Riga both also claim to have had the first Christmas tree—it's certainly true that Christmas trees' modern influence can be traced to Germany. As early as the 1400s, German guilds (trade and craft associations) were dressing guildhall trees with confectionary for children and apprentices, and they would dance around them on Christmas. The spread across the English-speaking world, however, is very much due to Prince Albert. When the cover of *The Illustrated London News* in 1848 showed a sumptuous picture of the British royal family's Christmas tree, it caused a sensation and was quickly imitated. By the 1920s, trees were installed in most homes of many countries, candles turned to electric lights, and today Christmas just would not seem right without a tree somewhere. Glistening with enchanting colors, there is something truly transcendent about a well-dressed Christmas tree, pulling us into a different state of mind—out of darkness and into light.

Christmas flora

Christmas trees tend to be conifers, such as spruce, pine, or boxwood. However, yew was used for a time—before its more poisonous qualities became something of a problem for children licking sticky fingers.

The poisonous berry of the European yew *Taxus baccata*.

Christmas Tree Controversies

Devout figures, such as Martin Luther, seemed to have no issue with using trees as a seasonal focus, with one appearing in the Strasbourg Cathedral in Germany as early as 1539, but some Christians objected to their suspiciously pagan heritage and resisted for a while. It took until 1982, for instance, for Pope John Paul II to finally introduce a huge annual tree to St. Peter's Square at the Vatican. Since the 1950s, starting with North American Lutherans, a number of churches have taken to creating "Chrismon" trees—the word is short for "Christ monograms"—and they are decorated exclusively with religious images, usually in white and gold.

Christmas trees have also been the source of some modern controversies. During World War I, there was a brief resistance to them in Great Britain due to their significant German influence. After the October Revolution of 1917, which outlawed public religious practice, they were completely banned in Russia, although in 1935 they returned (presumably by popular demand) as New Year Trees in a revised Soviet style, bearing the secular Red Star and overt state-sponsored decorations. By the 1960s, Christmas decorations in the shape of cosmonauts became popular, and New Year remains the bigger holiday in Russia today. The staunchly Communist state of North Korea, meanwhile,

BELOW: Perhaps surprisingly, studies show that the mass cultivation of real Christmas trees is less environmentally harmful than using artificial ones.

The environmental effects of Christmas trees

In December 2008, a Canadian study conducted by ellipsos inc. concluded that, once everything from production to transport was factored in, real Christmas trees grown as sustainable crops were less harmful than artificial ones. The researchers called the outcome astonishing, but found that in order for an artificial tree to have less environmental impact than a natural one, you would have to keep it for twenty years—and the average artificial tree is kept only for six. The growth of rentable living Christmas trees and widespread recycling plans has also helped reassure some environmental objections to using real trees.

reacted badly when, in 2014, South Korea decided to erect a stylized artificial Christmas tree on the shared border, threatening to destroy this "symbol of madcap confrontation" with artillery. (It didn't.)

Artificial trees have a longer history than might be supposed; Germany developed wooden representations using branches made of green-painted goose feathers as early as the 1800s, because of worries about deforestation. The practice soon spread to North America, and would give rise to artificial trees being mass-produced using brushes in the early 1900s. Some argue that fake trees are more environmentally friendly, because the ecological impact of the mass-growing of Christmas trees has caused debate in recent years. However, perhaps surprisingly, studies show that the environmental footprint of a real tree is actually far less than artificial ones in the long run.

World Tree Traditions

Christmas trees tend to bring people together, and large gifted trees are sometimes exchanged as symbols of goodwill between countries, standing proudly in many global cities and towns. The famous Trafalgar Square tree in London, for instance, is donated annually by the Norwegian city of Oslo in gratitude for British help during World War II. Tree decorations themselves have become another opportunity to internationally build bridges, with the setting up of the European Christmas Tree Decoration Exchange in 2018. This project encourages young children in schools across Europe to make and send each other their own regional ornaments to help spread cultural awareness of how Christmas is celebrated across the European continent.

There is a great variety of tree customs and many decorative styles across nations. Ball ornaments of one kind or another seem fairly universal, but other cultural slants are notable: paper and bamboo lanterns in the Philippines and China; seashells in Australia; spiders and webs in Ukraine (recalling a folk tale of spiders decorating a poor widow's tree); poinsettia flowers in Mexico; mock pickles and striped candy canes in Germany (the latter a trend that has spread around the world); and straw Yule goats in Scandinavia.

When to put the tree up also differs greatly. Germanic nations don't generally display their decorations until December 24 (their main celebration day), while parts of Spain and Latin America go for December 8 (Immaculate Conception day, beginning the period of Navidad, which ends at Epiphany). In Great Britain and Australia, some people often can't wait, going straight for the first day of Advent. Some Americans jump in even earlier, with their trees

LEFT: Poinsettia plants are a popular Christmas decoration in Mexico, and their popularity has spread to other countries too.

going up a week before Thanksgiving, which is always the fourth Thursday of November—in other words, pretty early.

When to take the tree down again largely follows the same rules for other decorations (see page 49), with equal warnings of bad luck if they are not adhered to. How much of a real tree is left when it has been up for nearly six weeks is another matter! Where fir trees are scarce, alternatives can be found. In Greece, for instance, the masts of tall ships are decorated, and in India some people paint palm tree trunks with seasonal images.

Christmas Dinners

Alongside the nineteenth century's growth of social conscience came a revitalization of the importance of family. While this was less of an issue among the wealthy, who had always been able to take time off work for domestic gatherings (if they worked at all), for those farther down the ladder, the family Christmas dinner took on new importance. With employers now granting at least one day off to the hapless masses (albeit sometimes reluctantly), the day had to be made the most of and the familial company enjoyed while it could be.

Just as back in the Roman Kalendae feast when "the poor also set better food than usual upon their tables" (see page 17), even those with very little would make more of themselves on December 24 or 25, saving up throughout the year to improve their lot for just a few hours. Critics of Christmas have always attacked the perceived overindulgence of the day, particularly today, with its impact on health and the environmental issues surrounding discarded packaging, trinkets, and trees. For many people in centuries past, and in parts of the world today, however, it was the only opportunity to have at least a small taste of luxury. The making of, and eating of, Christmas dinner can also be the one time of the year that family, close or extended, comes together and fully interacts. Although it may contribute to the odd family argument, if the spirit

A turkey coat of arms

The British turkey dinner is one of the most influential of Christmas feasts, and for that, we may need to thank one William Strickland, a Yorkshireman who first imported turkey to his home country in 1526. Strickland was a Puritan navigator who, on his travels, supposedly bought six turkeys from Native American traders and sold them for tuppence (two cents) apiece in Bristol. His descendants regretfully agree that there's no hard proof to confirm this story, but Strickland himself was evidently eager to promote it; his family coat of arms features "a turkey-cock in his pride, proper."

of peace and goodwill is adhered to, it offers the potential for an important annual bonding.

The uniquely nostalgic aroma of Christmas dinner being cooked can trigger some strong memories of seasons past. Naturally, the food eaten around the world varies enormously, but generally most countries enjoy increased amounts of meat and poultry, or fish, at the center of their Christmas celebrations. As vegetarianism and veganism increases, so other options are rapidly being created too, with nut dishes, vegetable pies, and roulades becoming more widely available.

Turkey has become seen as the traditional Christmas food, and is eaten in homes from Canada to the Lebanon to Brazil. However, the turkey frenzy some countries know today was not always thus. In medieval times, the Christmas platter was more likely to contain swan, pheasant, peacock, duck, goose, chicken, wild boar, or roast beef. Turkeys were first imported into Great Britain from North America in the 1500s and spread to Europe soon after. The first Christmas turkey is claimed to have been chewed on by King Henry VIII soon after its

LEFT: The Christmas dinner has remained the center of the festivities for centuries. Here, a Polish family gathers in the 1940s.

introduction, and by the seventeenth century it was gaining ground among those who could afford it. Goose would remain a seasonal staple of Great Britain, however, well into Victorian times, as demonstrated by Bob Cratchit's meal in Charles Dickens's *A Christmas Carol*. That Cratchit's gift from the reformed Scrooge is a huge turkey indicates the higher status that its more generous flesh was beginning to hold by then.

Christmas dinner around the world

Every culture has their own variant on the traditional feast. Some iconic dinners include:

ITALY: The Feast of Seven Fishes. Seven different fish are prepared in seven different ways, such as frying, curing, or preparing in sauce, and served throughout the evening.

THE PHILIPPINES: Lechon. A stuffed hog, cooked on a bamboo spit.

RUSSIA: Selyodka pod Shuboy, or "Herring in a fur coat." Salt-cured herring is layered under a salad of beets, potatoes, carrots, and eggs, making an impressive centerpiece.

COSTA RICA: Tamales. These are stuffed dough packages steamed in banana leaves, popular throughout the Americas—and you can expect each family to have their own favorite Christmas tamale recipe.

DOMINICA: Tripe soup. On this Caribbean island, where eating the whole animal is part of traditional cuisine, a hearty bowl of soup made from animal stomachs is a favorite holiday fare.

GREAT BRITAIN: Roasted turkey is accompanied by spherical, green Brussels sprouts and dinner is eaten while wearing paper hats from inside novelty "Christmas crackers"—decorative cardboard tubes that produce a loud bang when pulled apart.

"Bring us Some Figgy Pudding"

The strident demand "bring us some figgy pudding" from the old wassailing song "We Wish You a Merry Christmas" (see page 53) tells us that some kind of Christmas pudding was the festive dessert of choice for Great Britain and its territories several centuries ago. A dark, spiced dome of fruitcake, the British Christmas pudding is not as popular today, with reports of sales falling over the years; yet, to some, a Christmas dinner just doesn't seem right without one, even simply as decoration.

Rich, suety (animal fat) puddings began in England as savory, spiced meat dishes in medieval times, but somewhere along the line, as with mince pies—a pastry tart with a filling that was once actually made with ground, or "minced" meat—a sweeter tooth seems to have prevailed (possibly for a cheaper treat), and dried fruit, treacle (molasses), and alcohol became the main ingredients. The "figgy" and "plum" fruit puddings of Britain's yore have effectively become one and the same; in fact, plums were never actually used—plum was just a nineteenth-century British term for raisins.

BELOW: British Royal Navy "Wrens" sample the Christmas pudding in Scotland, 1942. Puddings are sometimes still a central part of a festive meal in British territories and have evolved over the years.

Despite these medieval prototypes, festive British puddings in the form they are recognized today didn't really turn up until 1714, through whispered reports of Great Britain's King George I being fond of them (he was sometimes called the "Pudding King"). The first seasonal recipes arrived fully formed in the 1830s, with one finally named as a "Christmas pudding" in Eliza Acton's *Modern Cookery for Private Families* in 1845. British Christmas pudding is usually served with custard, cream, or brandy butter.

While Christmas puddings keep well, due to their high alcoholic content, and can be prepared months in advance, there is a British tradition of Stir-Up Sunday. This is the Sunday before Advent in which the pudding is prepared, allowing time for the mixture to mature. On this day, all family members take a turn at the stirring, dropping in lucky coins or other tokens to find (and possibly break their teeth on) on the big day. It was said that the finder would enjoy wealth in the coming year. The name Stir-Up Sunday stems from the collect prayer in the sixteenth-century *Book Of Common Prayer* for the Sunday before Advent, which reads:

> *Stir up, we beseech thee, O Lord, the wills of thy faithful people;*
> *that they, plenteously bringing forth the fruit of good works, may of thee*
> *be plenteously rewarded*

Once Christmas pudding is served, there is another curious tradition: igniting the pudding with flaming brandy. While baffling to most people outside of Great Britain, it may have a serious origin. Some sources claim that the flame represents the passion of Christ and that there were originally

thirteen ingredients always used in the pudding mix, representing the thirteen disciples (if one includes Judas Iscariot). To earlier Christian minds, the decorative sprig of holly placed on top of the pudding thus becomes Christ's painful crown of thorns, offsetting the festive cheer and reminding revelers of the more somber cost of our salvation.

Note: Trying to light a Christmas pudding with brandy butter doesn't work—even less so if it already has custard on it.

Christmas desserts around the world

DENMARK: Rice pudding, known as *risalamande* (a word adapted from the French phrase for "rice with almonds") is served with whipped cream and cherry sauce. Families often leave a single unchopped almond in the mix; a small prize goes to whoever finds it.

GERMANY: Stollen (below). A doughy fruitcake seasoned with marzipan, nuts, and spices, and dusted with sugar.

ITALY: Panettone. A round, sweet bread loaf with candied fruits and raisins or sometimes chocolate chips.

JAPAN: White sponge cake decorated with cream and strawberries, for those who don't care for all those spices.

ISRAEL: *Sufganiyot*, essentially jelly donuts served hot. These are a Hanukkah treat rather than a Christmas one.

HONDURAS: *Torrejas*, bread fried in an egg mix and then baked in a spiced sugar syrup.

Games & Christmas Cards

As Christmas evening arrived in Victorian drawing rooms or more modest but still festive homes, sometimes risqué games of blind man's buff, squeak piggy squeak, or wordplay rounds were played, especially when the wine began to take hold. It wasn't the misrule of old, but it was an echo, at least.

Playing cards and mild gambling, usually for the men, would often follow as the night wore on, while the ladies sang or played music. Charles Dickens captures such revelries in the *The Pickwick Papers* and, naturally, *A Christmas Carol*.

How to play squeak piggy squeak

Everyone sits in a circle except the "farmer," who is blindfolded, spun around, and handed a cushion. The farmer places the cushion in the lap of one of the "piggies" in the circle, and sits down on the cushion. They then cry, "Squeak, piggy, squeak!" The piggy squeaks, and the farmer tries to identify whose voice they are hearing. If the farmer guesses right, the piggy becomes the next farmer.

ABOVE: John Callcott Horsley's design for the first-ever Christmas card.

By the late 1800s, in among the greenery and decorations, these parlors were sporting a new addition: Christmas cards. The exchanging of seasonal greetings by personalized means was ancient, but the concept of a widely distributed preprinted card arrived only in 1843, courtesy of Sir Henry Cole.

Cole, who also founded London's Victoria and Albert Museum of art and design, worked for the British Public Records Office (forerunner of the Post Office) and helped invent the "penny post" that revolutionized the affordable sending of letters. He initially commissioned the artist John Callcott Horsley to create a generic printed greeting to save him time each Christmas; the positive response encouraged Cole to make the card publicly available. After a slow start, and some criticism—the artwork showed charitable deeds being done, but a family raising a toast alarmed moralists because the smallest child was drinking wine—the idea caught on, and the industry of cards was up and running.

Interestingly, early themes often depicted spring flowers celebrating the solstice promise of warmer times, before December associations took over. Christmas-loving Germany was next to embrace cards; printed New Year greetings sent by businesses to clients and customers had already begun there about 1800 and, encouraged by Cole's success, Germany became one of the biggest manufacturers of Christmas cards.

When the Prussian immigrant Louis Prang arrived in the United States in 1850, he applied his background working with textiles and printing to cofound a company that produced lithographs (an economical form of printing). Soon, his enterprising ideas and knowledge of the English and German card markets would lead him to start producing Christmas cards for the United States in 1875. They quickly created a sensation across the country to become a major feature of the season. Ironically, Prang's success was also his downfall; as the cards industry took off, European competitors flooded the U.S. market, causing him to retreat to other printing work.

Fancy a game of charades?

Charades first emerged from eighteenth-century France as written riddles; in time, the game evolved into the more dramatic form of acting out. This was not originally seasonal but the game is often played at Christmas today (if now with the help of phone apps).

A Christmas Carol

If much of the paraphernalia we associate with Christmas began in the mid-1800s, what of the *spirit* of Christmas, which had been so crushed by the Puritan ban? How was that brought back into people's hearts?

It is widely acknowledged that the publication of a single story had a profound effect on how nineteenth-century British society approached the season: *A Christmas Carol* by Charles Dickens. This haunting tale of "a squeezing, wrenching, grasping, scraping, clutching, covetous old sinner," his disdain for Christmas, and his eventual redemption into a kinder, better man, has become embedded into the collective memory almost as much as the Nativity. The story's prose is moving, beautifully written, and genuinely scary—it is a ghost story, after all—and it captures the true essence of Christmas like nothing before or since. It is almost impossible not to feel a seasonal warmth when reading it.

Dickens's inspiration

A Christmas Carol was written in just six weeks in the fall season of 1843, and Dickens obsessively roamed the streets of London at night during this time, finding inspiration from what he saw and gathering the tale in his head. Subsequently, he spent years on tour in the run-up to each Christmas, giving live readings from the book.

It was produced as a novella by the Chapman and Hall company in 1843; disputes over the production costs and a bootleg edition that reduced Dickens's expected profits did nothing to dent its good intent and huge influence. Almost universally reviewed well, it was quickly realized by social reformers that Dickens had captured something crucial: the importance of peace, goodwill, and generosity even in times of economic hardship. It held up a mirror to modern society, and what was seen there wasn't comfortable. Its message was global. Many folk lived in hardship, while some who did have money, especially in the wake of the Industrial Revolution, were prone to miserliness. Hence the satirical figure of Ebenezer Scrooge, the central character of *A Christmas Carol*, whose cry of "Bah, humbug!" remains the eternal stereotype of the mean-spirited Christmas debunker.

The novelist William Makepeace Thackeray called *A Christmas Carol* "a national benefit, and to every man or woman who reads it a personal kindness," while the poet Thomas Hood wrote, "If Christmas, with its ancient and hospitable customs, its social and charitable observances, were in danger of decay, this is the book that would give them a new lease."

RIGHT: Bob Cratchit carries Tiny Tim in this image from an 1870s edition of *A Christmas Carol*. The story retains its power today.

For all its effect on the development of Christmas as we know it, it is remarkable how few people have read *A Christmas Carol* today. They may have watched it enacted by the Muppets or movie stars, but this is not the same experience. Something in Dickens's words brings his world uniquely alive and provokes tears of sorrow and joy. If you have never sat down with a copy of the unabridged book, it is something any Christmas lover or, more pertinently, hater, is advised to do. Turn the lights low, find a cozy spot by the Christmas tree, and absorb the pages. Only then will you realize the strong effect this tale had on its original audience and can still have today—and you will never feel more Christmassy. For all the transformations of the modern world, the themes and overarching moral remain relevant. Of the story's hoped-for effect on people, Dickens wrote: "May it haunt their houses pleasantly"—that it still haunts us today is testament to its power.

CHAPTER SIX

SANTA CLAUS

The Ascent of Santa Claus

If you do read *A Christmas Carol*, you may notice that the Ghost of Christmas Present, a full-bearded, jovial giant in robes and furs, reminds us of another character who was making his full emergence into habitual festive folklore around the time of its publication. It is time to come properly, at last, to Santa Claus—or Father Christmas—that personification of the season whose ubiquitous presence people now take for granted.

That this embedded trope doesn't appear directly in Dickens's tale and is merely implied demonstrates that the beloved bringer of gifts and good cheer wasn't yet at full throttle in this period of history. Although he had been slowly making his way up through the ranks of seasonal tradition, the true reign of Santa Claus, or whichever of the many names he has taken, was finally arriving.

If *A Christmas Carol* cemented the image of Christmas as a time of generous gladness in the public imagination, it was a poem twenty years earlier that gave the world another Christmas icon.

A Visit from St. Nicholas, better known today as *The Night Before Christmas*, was first published in 1823.

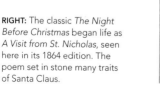
RIGHT: The classic *The Night Before Christmas* began life as *A Visit from St. Nicholas*, seen here in its 1864 edition. The poem set in stone many traits of Santa Claus.

A VISIT FROM St. NICHOLAS

PUBLISHED BY L. PRANG & C°.
159 Washington St. Boston.

Originally anonymous, authorship was later claimed by Clement Clarke Moore, but this was disputed. After the work was published in a collection of Moore's verses, the family of the poet Henry Livingstone Jr., claimed Livingstone was the true author. The debate still rumbles to this day, but despite whomever wrote it, nobody disagrees how important a piece of Americana it is—or of how influential it was in shaping modern Christmas traditions.

The tale told is simple. The narrator is nodding by the fire when a "right jolly old elf," Saint Nicholas, flies down with his reindeer-drawn sled, enters via the chimney, fills stockings with toys, and whisks away. The description is not precisely the modern vision of Santa—the character is "dressed all in fur, from his head to his foot," which isn't the fur-trimmed red suit of today—but the fact that he is "chubby and plump" certainly stuck in the public imagination. Santa, not always a hefty or laughing figure in his earlier manifestations, put on weight and became much more jovial after this.

As an interesting note, the reindeer were named Dasher, Dancer, Prancer, Vixen, Comet, Cupid, and . . . Dunder and Blixem? Those were the original names printed, and are the Dutch words for "thunder" and "lightning," but these days we know the last two better under the German names of Donner and Blitzen. Of Rudolph with his red nose there is no sign, only first appearing in a book by American copywriter Robert L. May in 1939.

Christmas in America wouldn't become a federal holiday until 1870, but the jolly old elf helped the country start shedding its Puritan reservations, and once he was part of the national consciousness, his influence would spread further. The origins of this kind of figure, though, go back a lot further.

Visions of sugarplums

The children of the poem dream "visions of sugarplums," but what actually is a sugarplum? Delicious though the idea sounds, no actual plums were involved. The term referred to a comfit, which is nuts or seeds coated in sugar; plum just meant they were round and sweet. Making these dainties by hand was extremely labor intensive, involving layer after layer of coating, and so sugarplums were a luxury item in their early days. By 1823, however, industralization meant such candies were available to ordinary children, even if only as a Christmas treat.

Santa's Many Guises

The academic view of this bearded, merry fellow is that he is a blend of several personifications of the season, principally the English version, who emerges from the 1400s onward and finally becomes known as Father Christmas in the seventeenth century, and the largely Dutch/American Santa Claus, based loosely on the legendary figure of Saint Nicholas, known in the Netherlands as Sinterklaas. He bears many names in different countries: Saint Nick or Santy in some parts of Europe, Père Noël in France, Olentzero in the Basque region, Papai Noel in Brazil, Dun Che Lao Ren in China, Julemanden in Sweden, Joulupukki (a humanized form of the Yule goat) in Finland, and Noel Baba in Turkey are just a few of the multiple variations, often obvious translations of Father Christmas.

Some countries have seasonal gift givers more distinctive to their own cultures. Iceland sees the visitation of thirteen separate *jólasveinarnir*, or

Yule Lads, over thirteen days. Russia and the Slavic regions welcome Grandfather Frost (or Ded Moroz —"Old Man Frost"—frequently seen in blue robes), while some Germanic and Dutch regions have Belsnickel (see page 122), a dark, grumpy character not unlike a male version of Italy's Befana (see page 32–33). In many areas of Europe and even Latin America, however, it

LEFT: The arrival of the Christkind, an embodiment of the young Jesus, who takes the place of Santa as the gift giver in a number of countries.

is the Christkind (*Christkindl*, or Christ child) who is awaited each Christmas. A tradition spread by German Protestants in the sixteenth and seventeenth centuries, this visitor embodies the youthful spirit of the Nativity Jesus (although he is sometimes personified as an angel). This has evolved into a hybrid Santa character known as Kris Kringle (an adaptation of Christkindl) in the United States. In truth, the international spread of the Western Santa Claus/Father Christmas, largely through his commercial presence, is gradually eclipsing the other mythological figures or merging them into composite characters. But then, he has always been something of a merged entity.

The Origins of Santa

The earliest reference to a great being who soared in the skies around the solstice would seem to be of the Norse god Odin, who led the ghostly Wild Hunt across the sky at Yuletide (see page 43). Later tales tell of his flying across the world on his curiously eight-legged horse Sleipnir, bearing gifts for the good, but, in some versions, abducting the bad. The multilegged horse may have become the multiple legs of flying reindeer and the Wild Hunt turned into a friendlier tour of generosity around the globe.

As to why reindeer might be flying in the first place, the shamanic cultures of the Arctic Circle—not far from Father Christmas's home at the North Pole—may provide an answer. The Saami people of northern Scandinavia and Siberia celebrate the shamanic properties of the *Amanita muscaria* (or fly agaric), an attractive red mushroom with white spots. Eating it can be damaging to health. The detrimental qualities were believed to be modified, however, if they were boiled, or, if the urine of reindeer who love to eat fly agarics was drunk instead. After this, the hallucinogenic properties of the mushroom may have made it easy to imagine that one was "flying with the reindeer" and the traditional red and white colors of Santa perhaps have more meaning than meets the eye. Shamanic elders were also known to climb into a yurt through its smoke hole if the snow had blocked the entrance, to deliver the mushrooms to others; one possible origin of the tales of Santa entering houses via the chimney.

RIGHT: The fly agaric mushroom, with its distinctive red and white colors, may have influenced depictions of Santa Claus.

Father Christmas vs. Santa Claus

That this chapter has already started intertwining the terms "Santa Claus" and "Father Christmas" is telling. Are they one and the same? In the West today, it would seem that they have become so, but it was not always this way.

The earliest personification of the season appears as Sir Christèmas in a fifteenth-century British carol, where the jolly japester is primarily concerned with bringing "good cheer" following the birth of Jesus instead of presents (which would become part of his role only once he began to merge with Saint Nicholas). A similar figure would feature in the medieval misrule festivities as a Prince or Captain Christmas, embodying the spirit of the season with high jinks and merriment as a chaperon or substitute for the appointed Lord of Misrule (see page 60).

ABOVE: British illustrator Robert Seymour's more pagan depiction of Father Christmas, with holly, wassail bowl, and Yule goat (1836).

Perhaps ironically, the rise of the British character Father Christmas came in the wake of the Puritan ban, appearing in more than one protest pamphlet. With the festival under attack, the act of imbuing it with a personality of its own made for a useful shorthand with which to make a point—that Christmas was an important presence in people's lives and was denigrated at great peril. Following the restoration of the celebrations, Father Christmas seemed to make a hasty retreat, his mission seemingly accomplished, and the character laid low, largely surviving in British mummers' plays (see page 66).

With the Victorian reinvention of the season, Father Christmas was revived and reinstated as the celebratory figurehead, although at first he looked distinctly pagan, often depicted as a bearded druidic veteran bearing holly, a Yule log or wassailing bowl, and even riding a Yule goat. With the nineteenth-century importation of the gift-giving Santa Claus, largely through British exposure to Dutch colonists in the United States, the distinction between Father Christmas and Santa quickly blurred, and the new hybrid character began his global spread. By the late 1800s, illustrations had lost the pagan influence and Father Christmas was as likely to be bringing toys and presents as offering a wassailing service.

ABOVE: German-born American illustrator Thomas Nast's more familiar Santa persona (1881).

Old Father Christmas

The oldest surviving record of Father Christmas's presence in folk performances, with one of the first descriptions of his physical appearance, is this 1780s verse from "A Play for Christmas" (translated from its Old English spelling):

Here comes I, old Father Christmas, welcome or welcome not,

I hope old Father Christmas will never be forgot

Old Father Christmas appears but once a year

He looks like an old man of fourscore year

Sinterklaas & Krampus

Who was the real figure behind Santa Claus? In truth, we know little about the oft-cited Saint Nicholas, the patron saint of children (among several other dedications), but his legends are many. As the Bishop of Myra in fourth-century Greece, Nicholas was renowned for his generosity, and most famously for throwing golden coins into the bedrooms of three impoverished sisters to save them from becoming fallen women. In medieval times, in memory of these good works, the eve of his feast day on December 6 was marked in some countries by children being given gifts. This tradition became particularly rooted in the Netherlands and, by default, Belgium (which split from Dutch rule in 1830); this is perhaps through the region's maritime connections with Spain, where some of the remains of Nicholas were said to rest.

Each December 5, the eve of St. Nicholas Day, incarnations of Sinterklaas thus arrive in Dutch cities, sometimes in a steamboat "from Spain," before mounting a horse (usually white) and parading the streets. With his bishop's miter and crook, Sinterklaas is a little more solemn than the jovial Santa he has helped give rise to, and is more of a tribute to the holy man his legend arises from. Controversially, Sinterklaas is usually accompanied by *Zwarte Piet* ("Black Pete"), a mischievous figure who climbs down

RIGHT: Sinterklaas arrives on a white horse in Amsterdam, Holland, in the 1940s. The Dutch version of Santa has a more sober air about him.

chimneys to spy on children and decide whether they deserve presents or not. Attempts to keep the polarizing traditional character without causing offense include "Smudge Pete," marked with soot, or "Rainbow Pete."

On the spookier side of things, in some European countries Saint Nicholas is also sometimes accompanied by the fearsome figure of Krampus, a horned demon that terrifies children with birch rods *(ruten)* and threatens abduction for the naughty. It is not clear from where this frightening companion, often displayed wearing chains and bells, originates, but he is almost certainly a remnant of pre-Christian paganism, which has somehow kept going as a balancing dark force alongside the more benevolent Saint Nicholas who keeps his worst excesses in check.

The tradition of dressing up as Krampus sees some genuinely terrifying (and sometimes sexually suggestive) beasts on the streets of some European cities: principally Austria, Bavaria, Croatia, the Czech Republic, Hungary, and parts of Italy and Slovenia, but the United States has also caught on. There have been attempts to reduce him to a more child-friendly character, after some Christian opposition to the devil-like representations. In fact there were actual bans on his presence in some parts of Europe in the mid-twentieth century, but the truly scary Krampus has resurged in recent decades.

LEFT: The darker side of Christmas. This image of Krampus, a seasonal demon popular in some countries, shows what happens to naughty children!

RIGHT: St. Nicholas, depicted in a Russian icon from Lipnya Church of St. Nicholas, Novgorod. His merging with Father Christmas helped create the figure of Santa Claus.

The Night before Christmas

As Dutch traditions were adapted by Americans, and Sinterklaas became Santa Claus (although, oddly, "Santa" is Spanish for a female saint; male saints are called *san* or *santo*), he then, in turn, merged with the British Father Christmas as transatlantic interaction increased. His role as global gift giver also grew, and the date of his arrival eventually shifted to Christmas Day itself.

On the night before Christmas, excited children across the world prepare for Santa's arrival. Where Santa leaves his gifts varies depending on which country you live in. Stockings or pillow cases on fireplaces or bedposts and other receptacles all seem to be acceptable to this remarkable being; in some parts of the globe, children leave shoes outside to be filled with treats. Santa is left a variety of food and drink on his nightly travels across the globe. A glass of sherry and a mince pie (see page 99) are left out for him in Great Britain, a pint of Guinness in Ireland, and a cold beer in Australia. To sober up, he has milk and cookies in the United States and a hot cup of coffee in Sweden. His reindeer aren't forgotten, with many countries leaving out carrots, water, or hay. In some Scandinavian countries, children leave out a bowl of oatmeal for the gnomelike Nisse (known as Tomte in Sweden)—another Santa equivalent.

The presence of chimneys in old houses provided the obvious point of

Getting ready for the day

SERBIA: Mischievous Serbian children have the option of a more direct route than trying to please Santa—taking their parents hostage. Gifts are given on the two Sundays before Christmas; on the first of these, they tie up their mother and release her in exchange for a ransom of presents. The following Sunday, it's dad's turn.

VENEZUELA: In the run-up to Christmas, citizens of Caracas roller-skate to morning Mass. Children often tie pieces of string around their big toes and dangle them out of the window; any strings noticed by the skaters get a tug, waking the children to come to church.

entry for the Western Santa. As they reduced in size, even as representations of Santa grew ever portlier, more ingenious explanations for entering the homes of several billion people all in one night were devised. Today, the science of quantum physics is used and a number of scientific websites, albeit with their tongues firmly in their cheeks, go to intriguing lengths to explain how all this might work.

The Proliferation of Santa

Although regional versions of Santa-like figures continued in pockets, by the twentieth century, Santa had become established as the primary Western personification of the season and the image of the red-and-white-robed, hefty gentleman rapidly took hold. Santa sometimes sits uncomfortably alongside Nativity symbolism, yet he is not in conflict with it either. Some religious observers have even argued that Santa represents a seasonal version of the traditional image of the white-bearded God. These two sides of Christmas have coalesced as much as Yule traditions were absorbed into Christian celebrations a millennium earlier.

One oft-quoted myth—and it is a myth—is that the Coca-Cola Company invented the classic red-and-white Santa with their Christmas poster campaigns, which began in the 1930s. While certainly influential, the fact that its corporate colors happened to match Santa's garb was just a coincidence: red-and-white depictions were established long before then and we have already explored one possible origin (see page 112) of the color palette. It is true, though, that the British Father Christmas was often seen in green robes in his earlier years, and the public pull toward red and white was made stronger by increasingly homogenized cards, posters, and advertisements. Russia and the Slavic regions have been more resistant, often sticking to Grandfather Frost's blue livery. This may continue an older tradition, because Odin, the ancient forerunner of all such characters, is said to have sometimes worn a blue hood. The green Father Christmas, meanwhile, has enjoyed minor revivals in parts of England, but there's no doubt red is the dominant costume of choice.

Is there a Santa Claus?

The burgeoning commercialization of Santa would soon see him splintered into many mysterious subpersonalities with suspiciously unrealistic beards, sitting in department stores and leaving a number of children wondering if he really was the same incredible wonder who would be whizzing around the world on the night of Christmas Eve. The most endearing answer to whether Santa exists or not was given in 1897 by journalist Francis Pharcellus Church to eight-year-old correspondent Virginia, in what became the world's most reprinted newspaper editorial:

Yes, Virginia, there is a Santa Claus. He exists as certainly as love and generosity and devotion exist, and you know that they abound and give to your life its highest beauty and joy. Alas! how dreary would be the world if there were no Santa Claus. It would be as dreary as if there were no Virginias. There would be no childlike faith then, no poetry, no romance to make tolerable this existence. We should have no enjoyment, except in sense and sight. The eternal light with which childhood fills the world would be extinguished . . .

No Santa Claus! Thank God! he lives, and he lives forever. A thousand years from now, Virginia, nay, ten times ten thousand years from now, he will continue to make glad the heart of childhood.

LEFT AND BELOW: Earlier depictions of Father Christmas often show him in green robes. After his evolution into the portlier Santa Claus, red and white dominates.

Christmas Characters

Santa may be the most famous Christmas character, but he is far from the only one: around the world, regional variations on familiar themes turn up for the holidays.

Some are kind and whimsical but others are grotesque and sinister. The German seasonal character, Belsnickel, for instance, is a scarier relation of Santa Claus, dishing out punishments to bad children even as he rewards the good. Old tales claim he would abduct the worst offenders, who were never seen again. Often portrayed as thin, crotchety, and masked instead of fat and jolly, the menacing figure of Belsnickel should have been enough to ensure good behavior from any child over Christmas. Darker seasonal characters may also have influenced Dr. Seuss's classic 1957 book *How the Grinch Stole Christmas* and some of the themes of the intriguing 1993 animation *The Nightmare Before Christmas*, which sees Halloween Town invading Christmas Town and kidnapping Santa.

Other slightly threatening presences include France's Père Fouettard, who whips the naughty children even as Père Noël (or Saint Nicholas) rewards the good, much like Krampus (see page 115). Then there is Perchta (sometimes Berchta), a Befana-like female figure derived from an ancient Germanic goddess, particularly popular in Slovenia and Austria. Although she is kind to hardworking children, leaving silver coins for them over Christmas (especially on Twelfth Night),

LEFT: The Christchild arriving at a house with Père Fouettard (sometimes known as Père La Pouque or Hans Trapp), a more sinister seasonal figure in France.

ABOVE RIGHT: Snegurochka, the snow maiden, in a painting by Viktor Mikhailovich Vasnetsov (1899).

she also has a less endearing habit of disemboweling the lazy and replacing their insides with straw and pebbles. This dark theme is further represented by the story of Grýla, the fierce child-eating mother of the Icelandic Yule Lads (see page 110), who lurks in a cave with her husband Leppaludi and their pet Jólakötturinn, the large black Yule Cat, sent out to eat any Christmas revelers who have not bought new clothes for the festival.

A more positive female Christmas figure is embodied in Snegurochka, the snow maiden. Derived from a nineteenth-century Russian folk tale, this beautiful young woman, said to have been made from snow by a childless couple (but Snegurochka would later evaporate into a cloud when unwisely leaping over a fire), is usually dressed in sparkling robes and furs and accompanies her grandfather, Russia's own Santa-figure Ded Moroz. Snegurochka is unique among these legends—no other version of Santa Claus has a female companion.

CHAPTER SEVEN

THE MODERN CHRISTMAS

A White Christmas

Snow has long been associated with Christmas, not least because this largely Northern Hemisphere festival occurs when the countries there are more likely to be cold and icy—hence all the snowmen on cards and in stories. Some families even fly out to visit a man who appears to be Santa Claus in the icy regions of Lapland in north Finland. Shifts in climate over the last two hundred years have seen snow become something of far less certainty in some areas, yet still people tend to look back to fabled "white Christmases" with moist-eyed nostalgia. Bing Crosby's 1942 performance of "White Christmas" is reportedly the worldwide best-selling record of all time.

Written by Irving Berlin for the movie *Holiday Inn*, "White Christmas" took on a life of its own once released as a single, and it would eventually inspire its own movie, complete with Bing, in 1954. Among those hearing the song were people who remembered, or carried the collective memory of, colder times when Christmas was often genuinely white. The period known as the Little Ice Age (from the 1300s to around 1850), saw centuries of freezing winters in northern Europe and North America, from where we get paintings of skaters and "frost fairs" on iced rivers. "White Christmas" thus tapped into the past, while forever cementing an idealized dream of what Christmas *should* be like.

Frost fairs

The frost fairs often depicted on Christmas cards were most common in mainland Europe, especially in the Netherlands. In the city of London, there were twenty-four full freezings of the Thames during the Little Ice Age, with the thickest ice (11 inches/ 28 cm) recorded in the winter of 1683–84. The last London frost fair occurred in 1814.

Christmas in Wartime & After

Another reason the comforting tones of Bing Crosby's "White Christmas" struck a deep chord in the hearts of many listeners was that in 1942 the world was, of course, at war. Hearing this song, service personnel stationed around the world in perilous places not of their choice were drawn back to where they would prefer to be, and could dream of more peaceful times past and, hopefully, ahead, while their separated loved ones did the same.

In times of war, Christmas takes on a new importance. In both world wars, belts had to be tightened, especially in countries where there were air raids and rations, so frivolity was inevitably reined in—but the need to celebrate remained. In Great Britain, presents became more practical or homemade, and ingenious alternatives to the usual seasonal foods were devised, such as roasted rabbit, or marzipan made from a mashed potato base. Sending packages to loved ones (often enclosing tobacco) was a crucial way of keeping up morale, especially in the first global conflict, which saw a reported 114 million Christmas packages and two billion letters mailed to war zones. Charities collected general gift donations to be spread far and wide to those away fighting, while the fighters in turn distracted themselves with simple decorations and entertainments, making sure that the time of year was not forgotten.

RIGHT: U.S. soldiers smile along with Santa in this poster from World War I.

Famously, a number of British, French, and German soldiers fighting on the Western Front held truces across some of the trenches during the Christmas of 1914, the first Great War. Although the stories have since become exaggerated, communal singing, cigarette swapping, and even impromptu soccer kickabouts were indeed recorded here and there. Authorities were unhappy, however, and growing public opinion viewed it as simple fraternization. Although the Christmas of 1915 saw a few more such gatherings, by 1916, direct orders had ended the Christmas truces.

The end of the next great conflict, World War II, left many European countries in a state of austerity that would see rationing linger on for years. But it would also leave other legacies; the annual morale-boosting Christmas Day address from the British monarch, for instance, first broadcast in 1939, would become a national institution in Great Britain that continues to this day.

As European nations recovered from social and structural devastation, and Germany, the land of so many seasonal traditions, was compelled to reconstruct itself in fundamental ways, North America began to take the lead in influencing the festivities. While some European children found themselves gumming together paper chains from old newspapers and still received homemade gifts, the United States experienced an economic boom that would see it leading a new arms race of more expensive decorations and toy manufacturing, taking over from the hitherto strong prewar influence of the German Christmas industries.

With a need to leave behind the gloom of the conflict years, much of the world was happy to look to the optimistic Americans to set an example of how Christmas could once again embody all that

ABOVE: Christmas parcels to those on the frontlines were crucial morale-boosters in both world wars. Here, U.S. troops in World War II are almost buried by them!

was good about the human spirit. Seasonally themed Hollywood movies, such as 1946's *It's a Wonderful Life* (in which James Stewart's character finds a renewed zest for life courtesy of a Christmas angel) and 1947's *Miracle on 34th Street* (in which the real Santa Claus—perhaps—is found to be working in a New York department store), warmed hearts and boosted people's self-confidence with modern morality tales that inspired society in the same way *A Christmas Carol* did a century before.

Christmas Shopping

The art of dressing a store or café for Christmas was already long established from the 1800s, but as electric lighting and mass-produced decorations blossomed throughout the twentieth century, entire retail malls became captivating, if occasionally artificial, attractions to pull people in.

As children in the United States, and eventually in an envious Europe, were enticed by glossy advertisements for bicycles, dolls, train sets, and toy guns, Santa was now being asked for more than he had been used to, and adults were being sold unrealistic Christmas dreams, too. The new affluence of mainstream America was having its effect. The more commercial edge that many people resent today and sometimes mistake for the original purpose of Christmas was taking root. Festivals had, in truth, been appropriated for commercial purposes of one kind or another as far back as Roman times, but as modern seasonal celebrations grew in scale, its takeover became more noticeable, and the pressures that Christmas can inevitably bring began to be acknowledged for the first time.

Yet the annual ritual of Christmas shopping (now launched in some countries by Black Friday, a sometimes controversial retail event that began as an American post-Thanksgiving sale in the 1950s) does have a curious appeal if you go about it with good humor—some stores are beautifully bedecked and

worth experiencing. Despite an increasing number of gifts being bought online, sooner or later most people will still find themselves bustling through the crowds in festive streets and arcades. The stereotype of the exhausted shopper at the end of a perhaps only semi-successful mission is familiar, but in the right mood, head held high and with a determination to practice peace and goodwill to humankind, it is possible to hum along to all the comfortingly predictable seasonal tunes wafting through the aisles and make it a positive experience.

LEFT: Children gaze longingly at the toys on display at Macy's department store in New York, circa early 1900s.

The Spirit of Giving

For all the concerns over the commercialization of Christmas, a fundamental goodness remains at the heart of gift giving. Toward the end of the twentieth century, the holiday season had settled into the celebratory patterns that people are familiar with today. Economic fluctuations have brought challenges, especially among poorer families trying to meet children's expectations, increasingly inflated by corporate and social pressure. But the value of thinking of others each December retains its currency, and volunteers give festive time each year to make the less fortunate happy.

Prowling the tinseled aisles can be wearing, yet the act of doing it can connect people to loved ones and fond acquaintances in important ways. Thinking of what would make someone else happy can be a chance to project beyond one's own needs and consider those of others instead. Christmas has long been a chance to think of others and many people give to charitable causes, but even if you are simply buying gifts, it is still an experience that touches the true spirit of Christmas.

Likewise, writing Christmas cards may give only a few moments of thought to those who will receive them, but it might be the only occasion in a while where the writers have taken the time to connect—and as they do so, they remember the place certain friends hold, or have held, in their lives. For all the predictions that digital communications would kill the Christmas card, sales have held up well. Their creator Sir Henry Cole (see page 103) might have been gratified to know that in 2001, a surviving print from his very first run of cards fetched an astonishing £20,000 (about $30,000) at auction in the UK.

RIGHT: To give, one must buy . . . Christmas shoppers throng New York's 34th Street in 1950s New York.

THE SALVATION ARMY
25,000
CHRISTMAS
DINNERS
TO THE POOR
MAMMOTH CHRISTMAS TREE
FOR POOR CHILDREN OF THE CITY

ABOVE: A Salvation Army volunteer braves the weather to raise funds for Christmas dinners for the poor and hungry.

A Blue Christmas

Christmas songs have a long history, with many modern favorites ceaselessly played around the world each December, some with more international appeal than others. Regularly voted the best Christmas song of all time in Great Britain and Ireland, "A Fairytale of New York" (1987), by the folk band The Pogues and the late Kirsty MacColl, manages to provoke tears of sadness and laughter while somehow remaining festive. And yet it's a sorry Christmas tale—a song of a couple drunkenly falling out.

However, it isn't the first sad Christmas song; "Blue Christmas," first recorded by Doye O'Dell in 1948 but made famous by Elvis Presley in 1964, and Wham's "Last Christmas" come to mind. Even the classic "Have Yourself a Merry Little Christmas," first sung by Judy Garland in the 1944 musical *Meet Me in St. Louis*, was a song intended to comfort a grieving girl, unhappy at having to move away from her beloved home and friends.

Perhaps there is a reason for such seemingly improbable successes. The acknowledgment that Christmas doesn't always run smoothly is a consolation to those who may face difficulties as December approaches and seemingly inappropriate seasonal fun erupts around them. Loneliness, want, bereavement, and personal challenges don't stop just because the festive bells are ringing.

While some people believe it would be best to bring an end to the celebration for such reasons, the Puritan ban (see page 64) demonstrates that the festivity would probably only reinvent itself in some other form. The truth is that people *need* a festival at this time, whatever you call the celebration. The ancients of the Northern Hemisphere knew well that a festival of light in the cold, dark winter was necessary to bring the hope of spring and renewal. The entire year orbits around it, providing a unique chance to briefly drop the numbing routines that can bind everyday lives in favor of something more frivolous, more loving (ideally), and more generous in spirit. But if none of the traditions suit you, this is also fine—you can do it your way. Some revelers retreat to hotels and cruise ships, with everything done for them, while others prefer to be alone and in peace. And it is always a fine idea to reach out to those who may need support through the season. Even a phone call or an enquiring knock at a door could make all the difference to someone's Christmas Day.

A Moment of Stillness

Christmas offers a rare but liberating breakdown of normality, with its glowing lights and colors, nostalgic aromas, distinctive food, and warming drinks. It also gives the pleasures of opening presents and watching others receive them, seeing the gleeful faces of children as they tear the wrapping off in a whirl, the healthy indulgence of having a little harmless misrule. If the thrill of Christmas has been forgotten, it is worth remembering the magic and joy many of us felt as children and seeing the festival through those eyes again.

If you stop to look beyond the paraphernalia of the modern Christmas and think about how this festival can make you feel, there remains a tangible aura around it that is easy to miss in all the rush. Children experience its purity the most, but without too much effort, the atmosphere of the season can still touch the hearts of adults. There is an undeniably distinctive quality about this annual nexus point. Perhaps something about the solstice itself might one day be identified to explain it. Maybe it is a subtle human response to the qualities of winter light and weather, or even the psychic accumulation of eons of focus on this celebration. The devout see the divine at work. Whatever it may be, there is something unique about the annual cycle we now call Christmas.

If Christmas is, in the end, a feeling above anything else, then it is worth trying to find a moment over the festive period to tune into it. This is not always easy for those who have to juggle entertaining, decorating, wrapping, and cooking, but if you consciously select a time to suspend all of that for just a few minutes, you can create a small eye of calm at the center. One useful opportunity comes in the early hours of Christmas Day itself (or Christmas Eve, depending on your custom), something churches tap into with midnight services. It is a time when a stillness starts to fall: roads begin to empty, revelers make their way home, and excited children are finally persuaded to sleep. A collective buzz of hushed anticipation, and a tangible quietness unlike any other, combine for a few hours as the Silent Night arrives. How, then, to best use this little window?

RIGHT: As people hurry home and begin to settle for the holiday, a special stillness seems to fall like no other time of the year.

To create a valuable moment of stillness, find a snug and tranquil place, perhaps by the tree, fireside, or crib, turn the room lights low, and just *be* with Christmas. Within a few hours, the delightful madness of the day will begin and another opportunity may not arise.

Your thoughts might drift to all the many different facets this festival has sparkled with over the centuries, from the ancients standing ready to welcome the first discernible signs of the sun's return, to civilizations marking the births of their messiahs or commemorating wild hunts across the sky, from the taking down of normal boundaries and indulging in unfettered celebration, to considering the needs of others and putting animosity aside. All of it has, in one way or another, been a celebration of light in the darkness. Whether people see that light as the radiant sun, astrological signs in the heavens, the Star of Bethlehem, the divine illumination of a son of God, the grace of Saint Nicholas, or the glow of Santa's sleigh as he rides through the sky, the message remains the same.

Each tiny glowing light, albeit just wire and plastic or wax and wick, can be a reminder that the smallest glimmer in the shadows can lift spirits and offer new hope for the future. This simple ceremony of rebirth each December, marked with laughter, contemplation, music, generosity of spirit, revelry, and feasting, has been a crucial support to the cultures that celebrate it throughout their many trials and challenges. There is no indication that this expression of determined optimism will be changing any time soon.

If too many plastic reindeer and all the commercial excesses of Christmas can distract from its wider good, we can always make the choice to turn our gaze inward to its real meaning—a meaning that you decide on.

A Very Merry Christmas

People don't always get to be where they would like to be on Christmas, and sometimes they have others to care for or can't spend it with those they would like to—or can't spend it with anyone at all. But you can get the Christmas you deserve in the best sense—in your heart and soul. For in reality, this is the only place where the act of celebration really resides, immune to outside influence. You choose. Christmas can be what you want it to be, wherever you are, and whether your celebration is grand or modest.

These pages have attempted to trace the origins and evolution of a festival that, for all the many forms it has taken, remains at the center of the year in many cultures and thus the lives of everyone living within them. Hopefully, in journeying through its development—and sometimes its travails—you will have found renewed worth in this strange and wonderful occasion that we call Christmas.

Whether you find yourself reading this outside of the festive season or, as is more probable, just before or during it, whenever it arrives, this author would like to wish you . . .

A Very Merry Christmas

JOYEUX NOËL! WESOŁYCH ŚWIĄT

Buon Natale! Καλά Χριστούγεννα

feliz natal *Mele Kalikimaka*

Frohe Weihnachten! Gleðileg jól!

Nollaig Shona Dhuit! *Zalig Kerstfeest!*

MERI KURISUMASU! Mutlu Noeller

GOD JUL FELIZ NAVIDAD!

Further Reading

Books

Ackroyd, Peter, *Civil War*, Macmillan, 2014

Brunner, Bernd, *Inventing the Christmas Tree*, Yale University Press, 2012

Daniels, Bruce, *Puritans at Play*, Palgrave Macmillan, 1996

Edwards, Ormond, *When Was Anno Domini?: Dating the Millennium*, Floris Books, 1999

Gilbert, Adrian and Bauval, Robert, *The Orion Mystery*, Arrow Books, 1994

Gilbert, Adrian, *Magi*, Bloomsbury, 1996

Hutton, Ronald, *The Rise and Fall of Merry England*, Oxford Paperbacks, 1994

Hutton, Ronald, *The Stations of the Sun: A History of the Ritual Year in Britain*, Oxford University Press, 1996

Lawson-Jones, Mark, *Why Was the Partridge in the Pear Tree?*, The History Press, 2011

Miles, Clement A., *Christmas in Ritual and Tradition, Christian and Pagan*, T Fisher Unwin, 1912 (reprinted as *Christmas Customs and Traditions: Their History and Significance*, Dover Publications, 1976)

Nissenbaum, Stephen, *The Battle for Christmas*, Vintage, 1997

Struthers, Jane, *The Book of Christmas*, Ebury Press, 2012

Tarnas, Richard, *Cosmos and Psyche*, Viking/Penguin, 2006

West, John Anthony, *The Case for Astrology*, Arkana, 1991

Wilson, Derek, A *Brief History of the English Reformation*, Constable & Robinson, 2012

Worden, Blair, *The English Civil Wars: 1640–1660*, George Weidenfeld & Nicholson, 2009

Websites

http://www.astro.com/astrology/aa_article160602_e.htm

http://www.benbest.com/history/xmas.html

http://www.historicuk.com/HistoryUK/HistoryofScotland/The-History-of-Hogmanay

http://sarahpeverley.com/2013/12/16/medieval-christmas

http://treesforlife.org.uk/forest/mythology-folklore/fly-agaric/

About the Author

Andy Thomas is a prolific writer and lecturer with an interest in history, folklore, intrigues, and unexplained mysteries. Andy is author of the acclaimed *The Truth Agenda* and *Conspiracies*, which explore paranormal phenomena and global cover-ups, and he has also written books on the history and traditions of his birth town of Lewes in Southeast England, famous for its huge Guy Fawkes festivities. His many other books include definitive guides to the mysterious and controversial crop circle phenomenon. Andy extensively writes and lectures in Great Britain and around the world, and he has made numerous global radio and TV appearances, including on the BBC, ITV, Sky, NBC, National Geographic, and History channels.

More on Andy and his work, with news on upcoming events, publications, and videos to watch, can be found at: www.truthagenda.org.

Index

Acknowledgments

Andy would like to thank: His very dear wife Helen for helpful feedback and patience; James Lawrence and Susan Kelly at Ivy Press for their confidence and enthusiasm; Denise Miller, Jason Porthouse, Richard Smith, and Jordan Thomas for their help and encouragement with the original project; Martin Noakes for partly inspiring the idea; and parents Ron and Heather Thomas for childhood Christmases.

Picture Credits